A Grammar Workshop

Grammatisches Übungsheft
für Klasse 7–10
von

Margaret und Detlef von Ziegésar

Lehrerausgabe mit Lösungen

Ernst Klett Verlag
Stuttgart München Düsseldorf Leipzig

A Grammar Workshop

Grammatisches Übungsheft für Klasse 7–10
von Margaret und Detlef von Ziegésar

Lehrerausgabe mit Lösungen

Quellen der Cartoons:

S. 8, 17, 35, 38, 54, 56, 57, 58, 63, 65, 70: *Punch*
S. 13, 50, 51, 53, 62: Gerald Manley, *The Piccolo Book of Cartoons*, Pan Macmillan Ltd.
S. 20, 26: Express Newspapers Ltd.
S. 42: PEANUTS Characters © 1952, 1958 United Feature Syndicate, Inc.
S. 71: The *Far Side* cartoon by Gary Larson is reprinted by permission of Chronicle Features, San Fancisco, CA.

1. Auflage A 1 14 13 12 | 2006 2005 2004 2003

Alle Drucke dieser Auflage können im Unterricht nebeneinander benutzt werden, sie sind untereinander unverändert. Die letzte Zahl bezeichnet das Jahr dieses Druckes.

Internetadresse: http://www.klett-verlag.de

Redaktion: Inge Schäfer

Umschlaggestaltung: Christa Janik, Stuttgart
Zeichnungen: Christa Janik, Stuttgart
Typographische Gestaltung und Herstellung: Eveline Wiest, Stuttgart
Satz: Lihs, Satz und Repro, Ludwigsburg
Druck: Gutmann + Co, Talheim
ISBN 3-12-511600-7
ISBN 3-12-511610-4 (Lehrerausgabe)

Inhalt

Abkürzungen und Zeichenerklärung:

jd. jemand
S. Seite
usw. und so weiter
vgl. vergleiche
z. B. zum Beispiel

⚠ Dies musst du dir gut merken, um Fehler zu vermeiden.

Hier musst du mitdenken, damit du eine Regel richtig ergänzen kannst.

Hier beginnt eine Übung, die du schriftlich bearbeiten sollst.

1 Present simple

Einfache Gegenwart

1. Bejahte Formen

I/You/We They (my parents)	**start** work at 7.45.
He (Dave) She (my mother) It (school)	**starts** at 7.45.

← Hier nimmst du einfach die **Grundform** des Zeitworts (z. B. ***start***).

← In der 3. Person Einzahl (nach ***he, she, it*** oder entsprechenden Wörtern) musst du ein ***s*** anhängen.

I **play** volleyball. — **He + s:** Andy plays basketball.

You **collect** stamps. — **She + s:** My friend collects stamps.

We/They **like** tennis. — **It + s:** Our cat likes mice.

Manchmal genügt es nicht, in der 3. Person Einzahl einfach ein ***s*** anzuhängen. Du musst darauf achten, wie die Grundform des Verbs endet:

I **go** to school by bus. — This bus goes to town.

We **catch** the bus at 8.40. — My mother catches the bus at 8.30.

Sue and Pete never **miss** the bus. — Martin often misses the bus.

British pupils **finish** school at 4.00. — In Germany school finishes at lunch-time.

Wenn die Grundform auf ***o, ch, s*** oder ***sh*** endet, muss ich es anhängen.

I **try** to help in the house. — My sister tries to help in the garden.

You **cry** when you're unhappy. — A baby cries when it is hungry.

Wenn die Grundform auf einen Mitlaut (***r, l, t*** usw.) und ***y*** endet, muss ich das ***y*** in ie/i umwandeln und dann s/es anhängen.

Aber:
I **play** – he plays — they **say** – it says — we **enjoy** – she enjoys — you **buy** – he buys

Nach einem Selbstlaut ***(a, e, i, o, u)*** ändere ich das y nicht. Ich hänge nur s an.

I **have (got)** one sister. — My friend has **(got)** two brothers.

Die 3. Person Einzahl zu ***have (got)*** lautet has ***(got).***

Beachte die Formen von *be*:

Langformen:	Kurzformen:
I **am**	I'**m**
He/She/It **is**	He'**s**/She'**s**/It'**s**
We/You/They **are**	We'**re**/You'**re**/They'**re**

Magst du Gedichte? Schreibe dieses Gedicht zu Ende. Benutze das present simple *der folgenden Verben:* come, line *(füllen, bedecken)*, shine, watch

Hast du Lust, dieses Gedicht auswendig zu lernen?

twilight ['twaılaıt] Dämmerung

The Night Sky

All day long
The sun shines bright.
The moon and stars
come out by night.

From twilight time
They line the skies
And watch the world
With quiet eyes.

(Robert Louis Stevenson, 1850–1894)

Wie sieht ein typischer Tag im Leben dieser Personen aus? Die folgenden Verben helfen dir, den Text zu ergänzen: catch, come, eat, enjoy, finish, get up, go, live, love, meet, read, send, sing, take, train, travel, walk, want, watch, work

Jennifer is a young tennis star. Every morning she gets up at six and goes jogging. After breakfast she goes to school. She trains for 3 – 4 hours every day after school. In the evenings she watches TV or reads a book. She travels all over the world to play tennis. Like this she meets a lot of people. She wants to be the world's number one tennis player.

Barry lives in London. Every morning he takes/catches the 8.40 bus to the bank where he works. At lunch time he eats sandwiches in the park. When he finishes work, he walks round the streets and takes photos. He sends his photos to magazines and newspapers. One day he wants to leave the bank and open a photographic studio.

I'm Suzette. I'm a pop singer. I don't really have 'typical' days. Sometimes I get up at six and go swimming. But on other days I get up at twelve. That's when I work until four in the morning. I sing in a band four times a week. We travel all over the country. My mum comes/goes to all my concerts. She really enjoys/loves them. One day I want to make a hit record.

Stell dir vor, du bist Filmstar, Sportler, Reporter oder …
Beschreibe einen typischen Tag in deinem Leben.

Lösungsbeispiel: My name is Janet Austen. I am a reporter for "Pop and Rock".
I listen to many records and go to many concerts all over the country.
Then I write about them. I interview pop stars, too. I like my job very much,
but I work very long hours.

Schaue dir deine Klassenkameradinnen und Klassenkameraden an. Was weißt du von ihnen? Wo wohnen sie? Welche Gewohnheiten, Hobbies, Wünsche und Pläne haben sie? Beschreibe zwei oder drei von ihnen.

____

____

____

____

2. Verneinte Formen und Fragen

I/You/We/They	**don't**	**like**	hamburgers.	← ***don't (= do not)*** + Grundform
He/She/It (the dog)	**doesn't**	**like**	hamburgers.	← ***doesn't (= does not)*** + Grundform (ohne *s*!)
Do	I/you/we/they	**live**	here?	← ***do …*** + Grundform
Does	he/she/it	**live**	here?	← ***does …*** + Grundform (ohne *s*!)

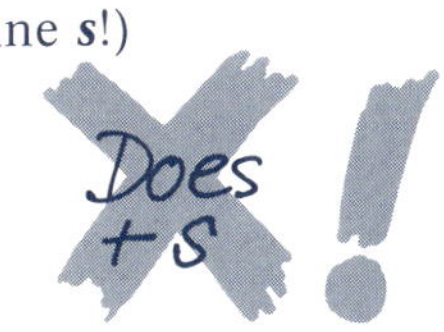

Das *s* ist schon in does enthalten.

Deshalb steht hier kein s!

I	**haven't got**	a bike.	You	**aren't**	on time.
Has Sue	**got**	a moped?	**Is**	it	late?

Bei ***have got*** und ***be*** benützt man kein ***do*** oder ***does***.

What can you say about Dave, John and Jenny?

 play table tennis
 play football
 ride a bike
 ride a moped
 collect coins
 collect stamps
 go swimming
 go jogging

Dave and John play table tennis. Jenny doesn't play table tennis. She plays football.

Dave and John collect coins. Jenny doesn't collect coins. She collects stamps.

Dave and John ride bikes. Jenny doesn't ride a bike. She rides a moped.

Dave and John go swimming. Jenny doesn't go swimming. She goes jogging.

Dave and John don't play football. They don't collect stamps, they don't ride mopeds and they don't go jogging.

Does Jenny play table tennis?

No, she doesn't.

Does she play football?	Yes, she does.
Does she collect stamps?	Yes, she does.
Does she collect coins?	No, she doesn't.
Do Dave and John play table tennis?	Yes, they do.
Do they ride bikes?	Yes, they do.
Do they ride mopeds?	No, they don't.
Do they go jogging?	No, they don't.

3. Verwendung des *present simple*

I **get** up early ***every morning.***
Martin **plays** football ***every afternoon.***
Our dog ***always*** **sleeps** on my bed.
Do you ***often*** **help** in the kitchen?
We ***sometimes*** **have** muesli for breakfast.
Julia ***never*** **forgets** her homework.

Das ***present simple*** verwendet man, wenn etwas **regelmäßig, immer, oft, manchmal** oder **nie** passiert. Es steht deshalb bei Angaben der Häufigkeit wie ***every morning/day/week/…, always, usually*** (gewöhnlich), ***often, sometimes, never.***

Schau dir die Beispielsätze oben an. Wo stehen die Häufigkeitsangaben?

Angaben, die aus mehreren Wörtern bestehen, wie

every morning/day

stehen meistens am Satzende.

Die Wörter always, often, sometimes,

never (usually) stehen meistens

direkt vor dem Verb.

What does the tramp say?
Benütze diese Wörter:
when/rings/the phone/you're in the bath/always

'Typical. The phone

always rings when

you're in the bath

_______________.

Das ***present simple*** benutzt man auch ohne Angaben der Häufigkeit für etwas, das immer so ist oder sich zumindest nicht so schnell ändert, z. B.

I **have** toast for breakfast.	← Gewohnheiten,
Becky **collects** stamps.	← Hobbies,
Wendy **drives** a bus.	← berufliche Tätigkeiten,
Do you **speak** French?	← Fähigkeiten,
Chris **doesn't like** maths.	← Vorlieben und Abneigungen,
Cats **eat** mice.	← allgemein bekannte Tatsachen,
This book **costs** three pounds.	← sonstige Tatsachen.

Sally, Carol and Jane live in a flat together. They all work. This is what they do in the evenings:

	listen to records	go to the cinema	watch TV	read books
Sally	often	sometimes	sometimes	often
Carol	never	sometimes	sometimes	often
Jane	never	never	always	never

Sally often listens to records.

Sally and Carol sometimes go to the cinema.

Sally and Carol sometimes watch TV.

Sally and Carol often read books.

Carol and Jane never listen to records.

Jane never goes to the cinema.

Jane always watches TV.

Jane never reads books.

I always/often/sometimes/never …

___

___

___

Warum steht in den folgenden Sätzen das present simple?
Schreibe als Begründung eines der folgenden Stichwörter daneben:

Gewohnheit, Hobby, berufliche Tätigkeit, Fähigkeit, Vorliebe, Abneigung, Tatsache

*(Manchmal sind verschiedene Begründungen möglich.
Benutze die Begründung ‚Tatsache' nur dann, wenn es keine genauere gibt.)*

Sandra **lives** in Vancouver.	Tatsache
Vancouver **is** in Canada.	Tatsache
Sandra **works** in an office.	berufliche Tätigkeit
She **writes** letters and **answers** the phone.	berufliche Tätigkeit
She **has** lunch in a small restaurant near her office.	Gewohnheit
Sandra's parents **come** from Italy,	Tatsache
and Sandra **speaks** Italian as well as English.	Fähigkeit
Sandra **loves** pop music.	Vorliebe
In her free time, she **plays** in a band.	Hobby/Gewohnheit
She plays the guitar and she **sings** very well, too.	Fähigkeit

Maybe she will be a famous pop star one day.
Who knows?

Kannst du ein paar Sätze über deine eigenen ‚beruflichen' (= schulischen) Tätigkeiten, Gewohnheiten, Hobbys, Vorlieben usw. schreiben?

2 Present progressive

Verlaufsform der Gegenwart

1. Formen

I	am / 'm		I	am not / 'm not		Am	I		
He/She/It	is / 's	**waiting.**	He	is not / isn't	**listening.**	Is	she	**talking** to Mr Brown?
We/You/They	are / 're		We	are not / aren't		Are	you		

Bei den meisten Verben wird die Endung *-ing* einfach an die **Grundform** angehängt:

wait + -ing = waiting

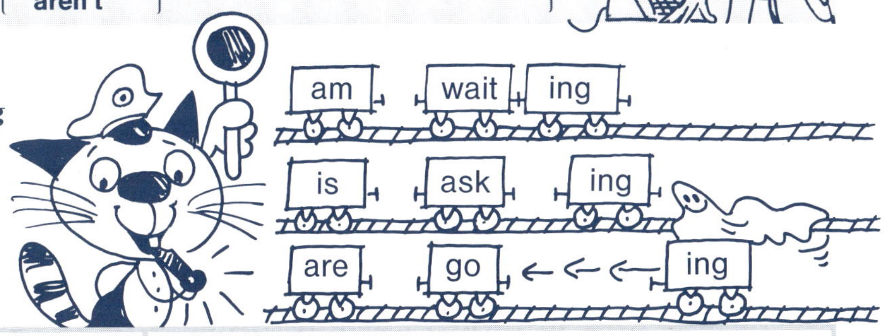

Beachte aber:

come	come + -ing (e durchgestrichen)	→ coming
make		→ making
move		→ moving
Lösungsbeispiele: write		→ writing
take		→ taking
drive		→ driving

Stummes *-e* fällt weg.

begi(n + n) + -ing	→	beginning
plan	→	planning
swi(m + m)	→	swimming
ge(t + t)	→	getting
put	→	putting
sto(p + p)	→	stopping

Nach einem kurzen Selbstlaut ***(a, e, i, o, u)*** wird ein einfacher Mitlaut verdoppelt. Dies gilt aber nur bei einsilbigen Verben oder wenn die Endsilbe betont ist *(**begin** – **beginn**ing,* aber: ***lis**ten – **lis**tening, **o**pen – **o**pening).*

lie → lying   die → dying

ie wird zu ***y***.

2. Verwendung

Das ***present progressive*** drückt aus, dass **jetzt/zur Zeit gerade** etwas vor sich geht:

Sue: What **are** you **doing,** Paul?
Paul: I**'m writing** a postcard to my friend.
Sue: But why **are** you **writing** so slowly?
Paul: Because he can't read very fast.

Jemand ist **gerade dabei** etwas zu tun.

The phone **is ringing.** Can you answer it, please?

Etwas passiert **im Moment gerade.**

Jemand hat eine Tätigkeit **begonnen und noch nicht abgeschlossen.** Die Tätigkeit muss aber nicht unbedingt im Moment des Sprechens ablaufen.

Are you coming?
– No, **I'm** ***just*** **waiting** for a phone call.

Is it ***still*** **raining?**
– No, **it's snowing** ***now.***

What **are** you **doing** in English ***at the moment?***
We**'re reading** a detective story.

Das ***present progressive*** kommt oft zusammen mit den folgenden Zeitangaben vor: ***just*** (gerade), ***now, just/right now, still*** (immer noch), ***at the moment*** (im Augenblick).

Das ***present progressive*** kann man auch für **zukünftige Ereignisse** benutzen: **Are** you **coming** tomorrow? Näheres dazu findest du auf S. 38.

Was ist im zweiten Bild anders als im ersten? Finde 12 Unterschiede heraus.
Du kannst folgende Verben benutzen:
carry, come, eat, fly, go, lie, listen (to), read, ride, run (after), shine, sit, wait (for), wear

1. In the second picture the woman is not wearing glasses.
2. She is not reading.
3. The woman's paper is lying on the ground.
4. The man and woman are waiting for a taxi. (They are not waiting for a bus.)
5. The man is not carrying an umbrella.
6. The boy and girl are not going into the shop, they are coming out (of it).
7. They are not eating ice-cream(s).
8. The boy is not listening to his walkman. (He is carrying it.)
9. The girl is riding her bike. (She is not pushing it.)
10. The birds are not flying. (They are sitting on/in the tree.)
11. The dog is not running after the cat. (It is only looking at/watching it.)
12. The sun is not shining.

3 **Present simple** oder **present progressive?**

Gegenwart oder Verlaufsform der Gegenwart?

Hier noch einmal die wichtigsten Stichwörter. Ausführlicher kannst du es auf S. 8/9 und 11/12 nachlesen:

Present progressive

Jetzt gerade (in diesem Augenblick)

My friends **are playing** football (at the moment).

Zur Zeit (aber nicht unbedingt in diesem Augenblick)

They **are building** a house. (Right now they aren't working. They are having tea.)

Present simple

Immer, regelmäßig, oft, manchmal, nie

They (always/usually) **play** football on Saturday mornings. They **don't go** to school on Saturdays.

Berufe, Hobbys, Fähigkeiten, Vorlieben

They **build** houses.

Sue **collects** bottles.

Mum **makes** the best cakes in the world! I **like** her apple tart best.

Kannst du beschreiben, was hier passiert?

A football player is leaving (leave) the football ground.

Welche Zeitform hast du benutzt? Warum?

present progressive – weil es

jetzt gerade/in diesem Augenblick geschieht

Und was sagt der Spieler?

'Goodbye – I always leave early (always, early, leave) to avoid the rush.' **avoid** vermeiden – **rush** Gedränge

Welche Zeitform hast du hier benutzt? Warum?

present simple – weil er es immer tut/weil es immer geschieht

Wähle zwischen present simple *und* present progressive.

1. Paul usually gets up (usually, get up) at seven. But now it is eight and he is still lying (still, lie) in bed. Today is Sunday.

2. Paul's mother usually makes (usually, make) breakfast. But today his father is making (make) it, because she is away.

3. Paul often goes (often, go) out on Sundays. But today he is helping (help) his father.

4. How do you know Paul's father is out of work?

(Because) he is reading ______ the job ads.
(read)

5. Paul's mother normally takes ______ the dog out.
(normally, take)

But today Paul is taking ______ him.
(take)

6. How do you know it is a warm day?

(Because) he is (only) wearing a T-shirt/he is not wearing his jacket ______.
(wear)

Zimmer erzählen viel über die Menschen, die darin wohnen. Hier siehst du Danny in seinem Zimmer. Schreibe so viel du kannst über Danny. Was tut er gerade? Welche Hobbys, Gewohnheiten, Vorlieben hat er? usw.

Wähle zwischen present simple *und* present progressive.

Du kannst folgende Verben benutzen:
collect, drink, drive, eat, have, lie, like, listen to, paint, play, read, ride, use, watch, wear, work with, write.

Danny is lying on his bed. He is watching (a football match on) TV.

He is wearing jeans and a T-shirt. He isn't wearing any shoes or socks. He is drinking milk and eating a sandwich.

He has (got)/rides a motor-bike. He wears a helmet. He plays football and tennis. He reads books and magazines.

At the moment he is reading "Moby Dick". He has a CD player. He listens to/likes pop music.

He works with/has (got) a computer. He collects stamps. He likes/eats a lot of fruit. He has (got) two budgies.

He is painting his room at the moment. He is (also) writing a letter.

4 Present perfect simple

Vollendete Gegenwart – einfache Form

1. Formen

I/You/We/They	**have** / **'ve**	**finished.**	They	**have not** / **haven't**	**started** work.	**Have** you	**posted** my letters?
He/She/It	**has** / **'s**	**gone.**	She	**has not** / **hasn't**	**left** yet.	**Has** he	**done** the shopping?

Es gibt **regelmäßige** und **unregelmäßige** ***past-participle***-Formen.

Finished, started, posted
sind **regelmäßige** ***past-participle***-Formen. Man bildet sie aus der **Grundform** (z. B. ***finish***) und der **Endung** -ed.
Verben mit regelmäßigen ***past-participle***-Formen nennt man **regelmäßige Verben.**

Beachte beim Anhängen der Endung ***-ed***:

promis(e) → promise(d)   move → moved
change → changed   close → closed

Wenn die Grundform auf e endet, hängt man nur d an.

cr(y) → cr(ied)   **Aber:** pla(y) → pla(yed)
try → tried   enjoy → enjoyed

Nach einem Mitlaut (z. B. ***r***) wird ***y*** zu ie/i, dann wird d/ed angehängt.

sto(p) → sto(pp)ed   plan → planned
drop → dropped   jog → jogged

Aber:
open → opened   listen → listened

Ein einfacher Mitlaut wird verdoppelt, wenn ein kurzer betonter Selbstlaut vorangeht (vgl. S. 11).

Gone, left, done, been
sind **unregelmäßige** ***past-participle***-Formen.

Sie werden nach keiner bestimmten Regel gebildet, man muss sie einfach zusammen mit der Grundform lernen. (Am besten lernt man die ***past-tense***-Form gleich mit; vgl. S. 22.) Verben mit unregelmäßigen ***past-tense***-Formen und ***past-participle***-Formen nennt man unregelmäßige Verben (vgl. S. 79).

Beispiele:

Grundform:	***past tense:***	***past participle:***
go	went	gone
see	saw	seen
have	had	had
come	came	come
do	did	done
be	was/were	been
leave	left	left
Lösungsbeispiele:		
begin	began	begun
eat	ate	eaten
give	gave	given

In diesem Rätsel musst du die past participles *der folgenden Verben in der richtigen Reihenfolge einsetzen:* break, buy, cut, do, drink, eat, finish, make, paint, wash. *In der senkrechten, dick umrandeten Spalte steht dann ein weiteres* past participle.

				D	R	U	N	K		
		E	A	T	E	N				
	W	A	S	H	E	D				
			M	A	D	E				
					B	R	O	K	E	N
		F	I	N	I	S	H	E	D	
				C	U	T				
					D	O	N	E		
					B	O	U	G	H	T
P	A	I	N	T	E	D				

The cat has ... all the milk.
Who has ... all the biscuits?
Helen has just ... her hair.
Kevin hasn't ... his bed yet.
Sandra has ... her leg.
Can I read your comic? – No, I haven't ... it yet.
John has ... his finger.
Have you ... your homework yet?
I've just been shopping. Look what I've ...
Don't touch that door. I've just ... it.

2. Verwendung

a) Das *present perfect simple* ohne Zeitangaben

John **has arrived** at last.
(Ergebnis: Er ist jetzt hier.)
Jackie **hasn't done** her homework.
(Folge: Es wird Ärger geben.)
Have you **read** this book?
(Frage nach dem Ergebnis: Weißt du, was drin steht?)

Wir verwenden das ***present perfect simple*** ohne Zeitangaben, wenn etwas geschehen (oder nicht geschehen) ist und wir uns für das **Ergebnis** oder die **Folgen** interessieren.

Was ist hier passiert? Was ist das Ergebnis, oder welche Folgen hat das? Schreibe zu jedem Bild zwei Sätze. Du kannst die Stichwörter neben den Bildern als Hilfe benutzen oder dir selbst etwas ausdenken.

Ergebnis	Ergebnis/Folgen
lose key	can't ...
He has lost his key.	He can't open the door/get in.
drop	lying on the ground/crying
She has dropped her ice-cream.	It is lying on the ground./ She is crying.
not clean	dirty
They haven't cleaned their shoes.	The floor/The hall is dirty.
someone, leave open	fly away
Someone has left the cage (door)/ the window open.	The bird is flying/can fly away.
forget the matches	make a fire
They have forgotten the matches.	They can't make a fire.

b) Das *present perfect simple* mit *just, already, yet, ever, never, so far*

The bus **has** ***just*** **left.** We'll have to walk.
Don't forget to phone Paul. – **I've** ***already*** **phoned** him.

Have you **seen** the new 'Supercat' film ***yet***? It's very good.
Have you ***ever*** **been** to Ireland? – No, not yet.

Don't throw the paper away, please. I **haven't read** it ***yet.***
Wendy is a very careful driver. She **has** ***never*** **had** an accident.

Do you know Peter Brown? – Not very well, I **have** only **seen** him once ***(so far)***.

Wir verwenden das ***present perfect simple***
- mit ***just*** und ***already*** für etwas, das **gerade erst** oder **schon** geschehen ist.
- mit ***yet*** und ***ever***, um zu fragen, ob etwas **schon** oder **schon einmal** geschehen ist.
- mit ***not … yet*** und ***never*** für etwas, das bisher **noch nicht** oder **noch nie** geschehen ist.
- mit ***so far*** für etwas, das **bis jetzt** (oder bis jetzt noch nicht) geschehen ist. ***So far*** kann auch stillschweigend mitverstanden werden.

yet
in Fragen:
Have you seen the film ***yet***?

already
in bejahten Aussagen:
I've ***already*** seen the film.

N° 1 N° 2 N° 3 N° 4 N° 5

Schau dir das Bild an und ergänze dann die Sätze durch yet *oder* already *und das* present perfect simple *(bejaht oder verneint) der Verben links.*

arrive | The school bus has just arrived.

get up (3x) | Have the boys all got up yet? – No, the boy in N° 1 hasn't got up yet, but the others have already got up.

wash (3x) | Have they washed their faces yet? – The boys in N° 1 and 2 haven't washed their faces yet, but the others have already washed them.

have | Have they had breakfast yet?

finish (2x) | – The boy in N° 4 hasn't finished breakfast yet, but the boy in N° 5 has already finished.

leave | He has just left the house.

Carol möchte eine Statistik für ihre Schulzeitung machen. Sie teilt einen Fragebogen unter ihren Mitschülern aus. Diesen Fragebogen hat ihre Freundin Tina ausgefüllt. Schreibe auf, was Tina schon mal gemacht und was sie noch nicht gemacht hat.

QUESTIONNAIRE

	YES	NO
Have you ever earned your own money?	×	
Have you ever been on holiday on your own?		×
Have you ever stayed away from home over the weekend?		×
Have you ever cooked for the whole family?	×	

She has earned her own money.

She has never been on holiday on her own.

She has never stayed away from home over the weekend.

She has cooked for the whole family.

Kannst du einen ähnlichen Fragebogen erstellen? (Er darf ruhig ein bisschen lustig sein.) Hier sind ein paar Ideen:

see a ghost

talk to the Princess of Wales

lose your head

rob a bank

write a book

be on TV

fall in love

kiss your teacher

have breakfast in bed

win a prize

ride on a camel

NAME: ....

	YES	NO
1.		
2.		
3.		
4.		
5.		

Gib deinen Fragebogen einem Mitschüler oder einer Mitschülerin zum Ausfüllen. Dann schreibe auf, was er/sie schon einmal oder noch nie gemacht oder erlebt hat.

1. ______________________________

2. ______________________________

3. ______________________________

4. ______________________________

5. ______________________________

c) Das *present perfect simple* mit *for* und *since*

Englisch: *present perfect simple*	**Deutsch: Präsens (Gegenwart), oft mit *schon***
I **have known** Frank ***for years.***	Ich **kenne** Frank **(schon)** seit Jahren / **schon** jahrelang.
Mark **has had** a moped ***since October.***	Mark **hat** seit Oktober ein Moped.
***How long* have** you **been** at this school? – For two months.	Wie lange **bist** du **schon** an dieser Schule? – Seit zwei Monaten.

Wir verwenden das ***present perfect simple*** mit ***for*** und ***since***, um zu sagen, **wie lange** oder **seit wann** etwas **schon** der Fall ist.
Mit ***how long*** + ***present perfect simple*** fragen wir, wie lange etwas schon der Fall ist.

Today is Friday. Frank **has been** in New York . . .

. . . **for** three days

SUN	
MON	
TUE	*Frank arrives in New York*
WED	
THUR	
FRI	
SAT	

. . . **since** Tuesday

For + **Zeitdauer:**
Wie lange (wie viele Minuten/Stunden/Tage/. . .) dauert etwas schon an?

Since + **Zeitpunkt des Beginns:**
Wann (zu welchem Zeitpunkt/an welchem Tag/in welchem Monat/. . .) hat der jetzige Zustand angefangen?

Kannst du die Ausdrücke in der Mitte in die richtige Spalte einordnen?

for . . .

for three days
for about two months
for half an hour
for ages

since . . .

since July
since 1990
since last Sunday
since you arrived

Fülle die Lücken aus:

Janey is a truck driver. She started driving a truck in 1987.
She has been a truck driver since 1987.
Or:
She has been a truck driver for (. . .) years.

Martin knows Andy. He got to know him last Christmas.
Martin has known Andy since last Christmas.
Or:
Martin has known Andy for (. . .) months.

Übersetze ins Englische:

Frank ist seit fünf zu Hause.
Frank has been at home since five (o'clock).

Du bist schon seit einer halben Stunde im Bad!
You've been in the bathroom for half an hour!

Wie lange hast du dein Motorrad schon?
How long have you had your motor-bike?

5 Present perfect progressive

Vollendete Gegenwart – Verlaufsform

1. Formen

have / ***has*** **+ *been* + Grundform + *-ing***

I/You/We/They	**have** / **'ve**	**been working** for hours.
He/She/It	**has** / **'s**	
I	**have not** / **haven't**	**been waiting** long.
He	**has not** / **hasn't**	
Have	you	**been walking** all day?
Has	she	

Achtung beim Anhängen von *-ing*! Manchmal ändert sich etwas an der Grundform (vgl. S. 11):

si(t) → sitting
ru(n) → running
writ(e) → writing
mov(e) → moving
l(ie) → lying

2. Verwendung

Englisch: *present perfect progressive*	Deutsch: Präsens (Gegenwart), oft mit *schon*
It **has been raining** ***since this morning.***	Es **regnet (schon)** seit heute Morgen.
I've been waiting ***for two hours.*** Now I'm going home.	Ich **warte (schon)** seit zwei Stunden.
Ken **has been talking** about his new girlfriend ***all morning.*** Here you are! **I've been looking** for you ***all day.***	Ken **redet schon** den ganzen Morgen von seiner neuen Freundin. Ich **suche** dich **schon** die ganze Zeit.
Have you noticed that car behind us? ***How long*** **has** it **been following** us?	Hast du den Wagen hinter uns bemerkt? Wie lange **folgt** er uns **schon**?

Wir verwenden das ***present perfect progressive*** meistens mit ***since...*** oder ***for....*** Wir sagen damit, **seit wann** oder **wie lange** jemand etwas **schon** tut oder wie lange ein Vorgang schon andauert.

Statt ***since...*** oder ***for...*** sind auch andere Zeitangaben möglich, z. B. ***all morning, all day.***

Mit ***how long*** + ***present perfect progressive*** fragen wir, wie lange etwas schon andauert.

Verwechsle nicht ***since*** und ***for***! (Vgl. S. 19.)

Since + **Zeitpunkt des Beginns:** since ten o'clock (seit 10 Uhr)

For + **Zeitdauer:** for ten hours (seit 10 Stunden / schon 10 Stunden lang)

(lawn) mower ['məʊə] Rasenmäher – **steadily** ['stedɪlɪ] ununterbrochen

Hier sind alle sehr beschäftigt. Was tun sie schon die ganze Zeit? Ergänze die Sätze. Benutze das present perfect progressive *der folgenden Verben:*

eat, knit, learn, make, paint, play, read, repair, write

Bei den Zeitangaben gibt es zwei Möglichkeiten: since … *oder* for … .
Sie sind durch einen Schrägstrich voneinander getrennt.
(Bei der zweiten Möglichkeit musst du ein bisschen rechnen.)

1. Diane has been writing letters since three o'clock / for two hours.
2. Tony and Bob have been making sandwiches for half an hour / since half past four.
3. Lisa has been knitting since half past four / for half an hour.
4. Jenny and Jeff have been repairing the radio for an hour / since four o'clock.
5. Pat has been painting since four o'clock / for an hour.
6. Lynne has been learning Spanish for an hour and a half / since half past three.
7. Stuart has been reading comics since half past three / for an hour and a half.
8. Julie and Steve have been playing cards for three hours / since two o'clock.
9. Neil has been eating crisps since half past four / for half an hour.

6 Past simple

Einfache Vergangenheit

1. Bejahte Formen

I You He She It We They	**started**. **finished**. **helped**. **came** back. **ran** away. **went** on. **drove** off.

Das sind regelmäßige Formen, … und das sind unregelmäßige Formen.

Regelmäßige *past-tense*-Formen werden so genannt, weil sie nach folgender Regel gebildet werden:

Grundform (z. B. start)

+ Endung ed. (Vgl. S. 11.)

arriv(e) → arrived   smil(e) → smiled

liv(e) → lived   us(e) → used

Wenn die Grundform auf e endet, hängt man nur d an.

cr(y) → cried   **Aber:** sta(y) → stayed

tr(y) → tried   enjo(y) → enjoyed

Nach einem Mitlaut (z. B. ***r***) wird ***y*** zu ie/i, dann wird d/ed angehängt.

sto(p) → sto(pp)ed   pla(n) → planned

Die anderen Formen nennen wir **unregelmäßig**, weil sie nach keiner bestimmten Regel gebildet werden.
Beispiele:

Grundform:	***past-tense*-Form:**
come	came
run	ran
go	went
drive	drove
buy	bought
bring	brought
find	found
Lösungsbeispiel: give	gave

Beim Verb ***be*** musst du auf die **Person** achten:

I/He/She/It was

We/You/They were

There was a young lady of Riga,
Who rode, with a smile, on a tiger.
They returned from the ride
With the lady inside
And the smile on the face of the tiger.

Welche past-tense-*Formen findest du in diesem Limerick? Wie lauten die Grundformen dazu?*
Ist es ein regelmäßiges oder ein unregelmäßiges Verb?
Schreibe „r“ (für „regelmäßig“) oder „u“ (für „unregelmäßig“) in die Klammer dahinter.

***Past-tense*-Form:**	was (u)	rode (u)	returned ( )
Grundform:	be	ride	return

2. Verneinte Formen und Fragen

I	**didn't**	**stay**	long.	← ***didn't*** (= ***did not***) + Grundform
He	**didn't**	**come**	back.	
Did	you	**enjoy**	the party?	← ***did*** + Grundform
Did	she	**go**	out?	

↑ ⚠ **Grundform** (nicht ***stayed/came/enjoyed/went***!)

Aber:

I/He/She/It	**wasn't**	there.		**Was**	I/he/she/it	good?
We/You/They	**weren't**	at home.		**Were**	we/you/they	in town?

Ergänze die Sätze durch die richtige Form der Verben links:

Last week Helen went on holiday. She enjoyed it very much. It was so different from her normal life.

get up  She didn't get up at half past seven.  She got up at nine.

have  She didn't have toast for breakfast.  She had muesli.

wear  She didn't wear her school uniform.  She wore jeans.

go  She didn't go to school.  She went to the beach.

be She wasn't inside all day.  She was outside.

play  She didn't play with her schoolfriends. She played with her brother.

 ride She didn't ride her bike.  She rode a horse.

watch  She didn't watch TV in the evening.  She watched the sea.

Folgende Verben helfen dir bei dieser Übung: buy, fly ✓, go, like, see, speak, take, understand

About two months ago Jochen won a trip to California. When he got back, he talked about his trip during the English lesson. Everybody asked him a lot of questions:

Did you fly? — Yes, I did.

Did you like flying? — No, I didn't. I was frightened.

Did you go to Hollywood? — Yes, I did. It was great.

Did you see any film stars? — No, I didn't. I was very disappointed.

Did you speak English all the time? — Yes, I did. No one could speak German.

Did you understand everything? — No, I didn't. Not everything.

Did you take photos? — Yes, I did. Do you want to see them?

Did you buy any souvenirs? — No, I didn't. I didn't have enough money.

3. Verwendung

My sister **left** school ***last April***.
There **was** a storm ***while we were on holiday***.

***When* did** you **come** back from town?
– ***Half an hour ago.***

Did you **collect** the photos?
(when you were in town)
I **didn't see** Kate at the party.
(last night)

Wir verwenden das ***past simple*** für etwas, das **vorbei** ist.

Man benutzt es in Fragen mit ***when*** und zusammen mit Zeitangaben wie ***two minutes ago, yesterday, last Tuesday, in 1990, when he came home, while we were on holiday***.

Der vergangene Zeitpunkt oder Zeitraum wird jedoch nicht immer ausdrücklich genannt, sondern manchmal stillschweigend mitverstanden.

Was ist aus diesen Menschen geworden? Setze die Verben über den Sätzen ein:

leave, get, not like, look

When he left school, Eric got a job at a bank. But he didn't like it. So he looked for another job. Now he is a circus clown.

finish, find, not be, learn

When he finished school, Brian found a job as a waiter. But he wasn't good enough. So he learned/learnt to cook. Now he works in an international hotel.

be, want, not pass, leave

When she was eighteen, Julie wanted to be a doctor. But she didn't pass her exams. So she left England. Now she works in a children's home in India.

come, be, not speak, decide

When he came to England, Hassan was twenty. He didn't speak much English. So he decided to go to night school. Now he teaches at night school.

work, not like, change

From 1989 to 1990 Mary worked at a supermarket. But she didn't like it. So she changed her job. Now she drives a taxi.

go, not like, move

Two years ago Carol went ______ to London. But she didn't like ______ it there. So she moved ______ to York. Now she takes tourists round the town.

leave, not get, go

Last year Barbara left ______ school. But she didn't get ______ a job. So she went ______ back to school. Now she is training to be an engineer.

Nicht nur Stars, sondern wir alle haben irgendwann einmal mit etwas angefangen oder etwas zum ersten Mal gemacht.

Schreibe ein paar interessante Fragen auf, die du anschließend einem Mitschüler oder einer Mitschülerin stellst, z. B.:

When did you learn to swim/ride a bike/...?
... write your first love letter/poem/...?
... get your first watch/bike ...?
... see the seaside/the mountains/a big city/... for the first time?

Frage:	*Antwort:*
When did ______ ?	______
When ______ ?	______
When ______ ?	______
When ______ ?	______

Nun berichte über sie/ihn (*z. B.:* Karin/Axel learned to swim five years ago.)

______

______

______

______

7 Past progressive

Verlaufsform der Vergangenheit

1. Formen

I/He/She/It **was** We/You/They **were**	**working.**	I **wasn't/was not** We **weren't/were not**	**playing.**	**Was** he **Were** you	**reading?**

Das ***past progressive*** wird ähnlich gebildet wie das ***present progressive*** (vgl. S. 11). Der Unterschied ist nur, dass du ***was/were*** statt ***am/is/are*** benutzen musst.

Also: ***was/were*** **+ Grundform + *-ing***

Weißt du noch, welche Regeln du beim Anhängen von *-ing* an die Grundform beachten musst? Wenn du nicht mehr ganz sicher bist, schau lieber nochchmal auf S. 11 nach, bevor du die folgende Übung machst.

Schreibe die -ing-*Form zu folgenden Verben auf:*

come	coming	write	writing	die	dying	plan	planning
get	getting	move	moving	open	opening	stay	staying
lie	lying	begin	beginning	change	changing	sit	sitting

Das *past progressive* ist, wie du siehst, ganz einfach zu bilden. Aber es wird viel seltener benutzt als das ***past simple***.

Welche past-*Formen enthält dieser Limerick?*

past simple: was, dreamed, woke (up), found, was

past progressive: was eating

fright Schreck – **perfectly** absolut

2. Verwendung

What **were** you **doing *at six last night***? You didn't answer the phone. – I **was working** in the garden. ***When I got up this morning***, it **was raining**.

While I **was having** a shower, the telephone **rang**. What **were** you **doing** when you **broke** your arm? – I **was riding** my bike.

Mit dem ***past progressive*** können wir sagen, was **zu einem bestimmten Zeitpunkt** der Vergangenheit **gerade vor sich ging**.

Wenn ein Vorgang durch ein neues Ereignis unterbrochen wurde, benutzen wir für den **unterbrochenen Vorgang** das ***past progressive*** und für das **neue Ereignis** das ***past simple***.

comfortable [ˈkʌmfətəbl] bequem

Why didn't they hear the door bell?
Benutze diese Verben:
have, listen, make, play, sing, wash

Dave was having a shower.

John was listening to CDs.

Mandy was making a phone call.

Linda was washing her hair.

Sue was playing the guitar.

Pete and Debbie were singing.

Yesterday morning rich old Mr Moneybags was murdered. The police found out that he was killed at 10.30.

Inspector Ann Harding is now interviewing everyone in the house: his wife, his son Andrew and his daughter Lavinia, Mrs Kleenit, the housekeeper, Mr Speedy, the chauffeur and Mr Green, the gardener.

Was sagen die Leute? Benutze die Verben in Klammern.

What were you doing (do) at half past ten yesterday?

Mrs Moneybags

I was writing (write) some letters in my room. Mrs Kleenit brought me a cup of tea at quarter past ten. I was just putting (put) on the stamps then.

Lavinia

I was talking (talk) to a friend on the phone. She rang me up some time after ten. At twenty to eleven I looked at my watch. I had to hang up, because I had to get ready for my tennis lesson at eleven. But at 10.30 we were still talking (talk).

Andrew

I was driving (drive) my father's Rolls Royce to town. He had asked me to take a letter to his bank. I left at 10.15 and came back at eleven.

Mrs Kleenit

I was getting (get) lunch ready. But I took Mrs and Mr Moneybags a cup of tea each at quarter past ten. Mr Moneybags was all right then. He was working (work) in his room.

Mr Green

Mr Speedy

I was cleaning (clean) Mr Moneybags' Rolls Royce in front of the garage. Mr Green saw me from the garden, where he was cutting (cut) down a tree.

I was cutting (cut) down an old tree. Mr Speedy saw me doing it. He was working (work) on Mr Moneybags' car in front of the garage.

After the interviews Inspector Harding knows who probably killed Mr Moneybags. Do you?

8 Present perfect oder past simple?

Vollendete Gegenwart oder einfache Vergangenheit?

1. Interessiert man sich für das Ergebnis oder für die näheren Umstände der Handlung?

Present perfect simple	***Past simple***
Kevin **has broken** his leg. He can't play football next week.	Kevin **broke** his leg *when he went skiing.*
Nur die Tatsache, dass das Bein gebrochen ist und die Folgen sind wichtig. Wann oder wie es geschah ist unwesentlich.	Es ist von Interesse, wann und wie es geschah, nämlich beim Skifahren.
Has Ali **left** school?	*When* **did** Eileen **leave** school?
Von Interesse ist nur, ob Ali noch zur Schule geht oder nicht.	Am wichtigsten ist der Zeitpunkt: **wann** sie die Schule verlassen hat.
Have you ever **talked** to a film star? – No, I **have** never **met** one.	I **met** Brenda *on the bus on my way home from school.* – **Did** you **talk** to her?
Wichtig ist nur, ob etwas überhaupt schon geschehen ist. Der Zeitpunkt ist uninteressant.	Der Ort der Handlung ist wichtig. Die Zeit wird stillschweigend mitverstanden (nach der Schule).
Nur das Ergebnis oder die Folgen sind wichtig – der Zeitpunkt der Handlung ist unwichtig	**Die näheren Umstände der Handlung sind wichtig: wann, wo oder wie**

The Grand Hotel **has burnt** down completely. The fire **broke** out *on the first floor last night.* One of the hotel guests **noticed** a funny smell and **rang** up the reception. But...

Viele Texte beginnen im ***present perfect*** und werden im ***past simple*** fortgeführt: Zuerst wird nur die Tatsache erwähnt, **dass** etwas geschehen ist ***(present perfect)***. Dann folgen die näheren Umstände der Handlung wie Zeit und Ort ***(past simple)***.

Have a laugh!

Jimmy: Has anyone lost 50p?
Jane: Yes, me.
Jimmy: Where did you lose it?
Jane: Where you found it.

Jill: Daddy, Jack's broken my doll.
Daddy: How did he do that?
Jill: I hit him on the head with it.

doll [dɒl] Puppe

Farmer Brown: That was a terrible storm we had last night, wasn't it? Did it damage your barn?
Farmer Giles: I don't know. I haven't found it yet.

barn Scheune

Ergänze die folgenden Sätze. Benutze entweder das present perfect *oder das* past simple *der Verben in Klammern. Wenn du dich für das* past simple *entscheidest, dann unterstreiche die Wörter, die dir bei deiner Wahl geholfen haben.*

1. I haven't written (not write) to my pen friend yet this year. Last year I wrote (write) one letter every month.
2. Have you seen (see) the new 'Supercat' film yet? – Yes, I saw (see) it last Saturday.
3. I lost (lose) another biro yesterday. I have lost (lose) three biros this week!
4. Have you met (meet) Linda's new boyfriend yet? – Yes, I met (meet) him at her birthday party.
5. It's 11 pm and Helen hasn't come (not come) home yet. The concert finished (finish) at 9.30.
6. Last night Helen didn't come (not come) home until after midnight. She was (be) out with friends.
7. Have you had (have) lunch yet? – Yes, I had (have) a sandwich in town.
8. Have you ever been (be) in real danger? – Yes, once, during the winter holidays. My dad and I lost (lose) our way in the mountains when it started (start) snowing.
9. The new disco opened (open) last Saturday. – Yes, I read (read) about it in the newspaper.
10. Have you written (write) your Christmas cards yet? – No, I haven't had (not have) time so far.

2. Dauert das Geschehen noch an oder ist es vorbei?

Es dauert noch an: ***present perfect*** **mit** ***since …, for …, how long***	**Es ist vorbei:** ***past simple*** **(meist mit Zeitangabe der Vergangenheit)**
Sue **hasn't been** to school ***since Monday***. She **has been** ill ***for a week***. (Sie geht immer noch nicht zur Schule, weil sie immer noch krank ist.)	Chris **didn't go** to school ***last week***. He **was** ill. (Er ist nicht mehr krank und geht jetzt wieder zur Schule.)
How long **have** you **had** your hamster? (Er/Sie hat den Hamster noch.)	I ***once*** **had** a hamster, but it died. (Er/Sie hat keinen Hamster mehr.)

Übersetze die Sätze in der linken Spalte ins Deutsche:

Sue geht seit Montag nicht zur Schule. Sie ist seit einer Woche krank.

Wie lange hast du/habt ihr euren Hamster schon?

Was fällt dir auf?

Im Deutschen benutzt man, wenn etwas noch andauert, die Gegenwart/das Präsens.

Setze das present perfect *oder das* past simple *der Verben in Klammern ein:*

1. Dave has been (be) in our class since Easter. He came (come) to live here about two months ago.
2. How long have you known (know) your friend? – I met (meet) her a year ago.
3. I like your new pullover. – It isn't new. I 've had (have) it for years. My aunt gave (give) it to me for my fourteenth birthday. She knitted (knit) it herself.

9 Past perfect
Vorvergangenheit

1. Formen

I/You/He/She/It/We/They	'd had	**finished.** **gone.**	He	**hadn't** **had not**	**noticed** us. **seen** us.	**Had** it	**changed?** **grown?**

↑ ↑

had (Kurzform: ***'d***) + ***past participle***

Weißt du noch, wie das ***past participle*** gebildet wird? Wenn nicht, schau nach auf S. 13.

Schreibe ein paar Beispiele für regelmäßige und unregelmäßige past-participle-*Formen auf.*

Lösungsbeipiele:

Regelmäßig: finished, noticed, changed Unregelmäßig: gone, seen, grown

2. Verwendung

After I **had written** all my letters I *went* for a walk.
When we *arrived* at the cinema last night, the film **had *already* started.**
Andy **had *just* gone** out when his girlfriend *phoned*.

Mit dem ***past perfect*** drücken wir aus, dass etwas schon **vor** einem anderen vergangenen Ereignis geschehen war. (Für das andere vergangene Ereignis benutzen wir das ***past simple***.)
Adverbien wie ***already, just*** und ***never*** stehen zwischen ***had*** und dem ***past participle.***

Was geschah zuerst? Erkläre den Unterschied zwischen folgenden beiden Sätzen: kam er an / gingen alle

1. When he arrived at the party, everyone **had left**, except one. Zuerst gingen alle, dann kam er an.
2. When he arrived at the party, everyone **left**, except one. Zuerst kam er an, dann gingen alle.

Zu welchem Satz passt diese Zeichnung? 2

Kannst du eine Zeichnung zum anderen Satz machen?

Ergänze die Sätze durch das past simple *oder das* past perfect *der Verben in Klammern.*

1. When we arrived at the station, the train had left (leave), so we took the bus.
2. When Mr Brown came home from work, he took (take) off his coat and turned (turn) on the radio.
3. When the firemen arrived, it was too late: the house had burnt/burned (burn) down.
4. When little Peggy cut her finger, she cried (cry).

Last summer Carol saw an advertisement for a bus tour of Italy. She had always wanted to go to Italy. She phoned some of her friends to ask them to go with her.

When she rang Pauline and Christine,

they *had just left* for France.

When she asked Tessa,

she had already booked her holidays.

When she went to see Ann,

she had decided to stay at home.

So Carol decided to go alone. But then, when she went to the travel agency,

they had (already) sold all the tickets.

Last summer Ben went to stay with his penfriend in New Mexico. For the first time in his life he drove through a desert. He saw some Indian dances. He ate Indian food. He rode a horse, and he flew in a helicopter.

Before he went to New Mexico, he *had* never

driven through a desert.

He had never seen any Indian dances.

He had never eaten Indian food.

He had never ridden a horse,

and he had never flown

in a helicopter.

And you? *Schreibe ein paar Sätze über dich selbst in dieser Art:*
Before I came/went to ..., I had never ...

10 Going to-future

Die Zukunft mit *going to*

1. Formen

I	**'m**	**going to**	**leave.**	I	**'m not**	**going to stay.**	What	**am**	I	**going to do?**
We/You/They	**'re**			We	**aren't**			**are**	you	
He/She/It	**'s**			He	**isn't**			**is**	she	

Kurzformen von **↑** *am/are/is* + **↑** *going to* + **↑** **Grundform**

Natürlich kann man auch die Langformen von *be* benutzen,

z. B. 'I am going to', 'we are going to',

aber in der Umgangssprache sind die Kurzformen viel üblicher.

2. Verwendung

Carol and John **are going to learn** Italian.
They**'re going to work** in Italy.
(... haben vor, Italienisch zu lernen. Sie haben die Absicht, in Italien zu arbeiten.)

What **are** you **going to do** in the summer holidays? – **I'm going to get** a job.
(Was **machst** du in den Sommerferien? – Ich **suche** mir einen Job.)

Mit ***going to*** können wir eine **Absicht**, einen **Plan** für die Zukunft ausdrücken.

Achtung:
Im Deutschen benutzen wir für eine Absicht oft das Präsens (die Gegenwart). Im Englischen darfst du hier auf keinen Fall das ***present simple*** verwenden.

What are these people going to do?
Hier sind ein paar Wörter, die dir bei der Lösung helfen:
buy, have, make, read, ride, see — bikes, book, film, ice-cream, phone call, shower

He *is going to* make a phone call.

She is going to buy an ice-cream.

She is going to read a book.

They are going to see a film.

They are going to ride

their bikes.

He is going to have a shower.

And you? What are you going to do this evening/at the weekend/on ... ?

And what about your plans for the future? What are you (not) going to do when you leave school/when you're eighteen/when you're older/... ?

Will-future

Die Zukunft mit *will*

1. Formen

I/You/He/She/It/We/They	**'ll** / **will**	**ring** later.	He	**won't** / **will not**	**come.**	**Will** we **be** on time?

↑ *will* + ↑ Grundform/Infinitiv

(Sicher weißt du, wie wir diese Form in den vorangehenden Kapiteln immer genannt haben.)

2. Verwendung

a) *Will* für spontane Entschlüsse

The phone's ringing. – **I'll answer** it.
I can't do my homework. – **I'll help** you.
This suitcase is so heavy. – **I'll carry** it for you.

Linda's in hospital. – Oh, is she? **I'll visit** her tomorrow afternoon.
(Ich **besuche** sie morgen Nachmittag.)

Will benutzen wir, wenn wir uns **spontan,** d. h. im Moment des Sprechens, zu etwas entschließen, z. B. jemandem zu helfen.

Achtung: Im Deutschen benutzen wir hier oft die Gegenwart (das Präsens). Im Englischen darf man das ***present simple*** hier **nicht** verwenden.

You are planning a day at Eurodisney with some friends. Everyone has to help with the organization.
Ergänze die Dialoge. Du kannst folgende Verben verwenden: ask, bring, check, find, make, take

b) *Will* für Vermutungen und Erwartungen

Sue **will be** eighteen next year.
I **won't be** home before five, so ring me later.
I expect Craig **will be** late again tonight.
He**'ll *probably* miss** the bus, as usual.
We ***probably* won't get** any tickets.

Will benutzen wir, wenn wir **wissen** oder **vermuten**, dass etwas geschehen wird.
Will wird oft in Verbindung mit ***I expect*** und ***probably*** gebraucht.
Aufgepasst! *Probably* steht **vor *won't*.**

Was sagst du in den folgenden Situationen?
Benutze die Wörter in Klammern.

1. You and your friend are going home on the bus. You wanted to watch a football match on TV.

   It starts at seven. Your watch says six fifty-five.

   You say, "We won't see (see) the beginning of the match."

2. Your friend is afraid of the exam. But he or she has worked very hard for it.

   You say, "Don't worry. It 'll be (be) all right. You 'll probably get (probably – get) the best marks."

3. Your friend wants tickets for a concert. You have seen this notice:

   You say, "We won't get (get) any tickets."

4. Your friend has got a new job in a different country.

   You say, "We probably won't see (probably – see) each other again. I 'll miss (miss) you."

5. Your friend has forgotten to buy his or her sister a birthday present.

   You say, "She won't mind (mind). She 'll understand (understand). Why not take her to the cinema instead?"

'I'll be sorry when he leaves home – he's such a damn good navigator.'

damn [dæm] verdammt
navigator [ˈnævɪgeɪtə] Lotse

c) *Will* vor Nebensätzen mit *as soon as, until, when*

Im Hauptsatz: *will*	Im Nebensatz: *present simple/present perfect*
I**'ll ring** you	***as soon as*** I **get** home.
We **won't leave**	***until*** it **stops** raining.
I**'ll come**	***when*** I**'ve finished** my tea.

Wenn wir über die Zukunft reden und Nebensätze mit ***as soon as, until*** oder ***when*** gebrauchen, steht im Hauptsatz ***will.***

Im Nebensatz steht jedoch das ***present simple*** oder das ***present perfect.***

(Zu Nebensätzen mit ***if*** siehe S. 41.)

Ich **warte**, bis er **kommt**. — Im Deutschen steht im Hauptsatz die Gegenwart.

I'**ll wait** until he **comes**. — Im Englischen steht im Hauptsatz das will-future.

Diane is going to stay with a German family. Her sister, Helen, has been there before.
This is what Diane's family says before she leaves.

*Setze das **will-future** oder das **present simple** der Verben in Klammern ein.*

Mum: You 'll let (let) us know when you get (get) there, won't you?

Diane: Yes, Mum. I 'll write (write) to you as soon as I arrive (arrive).

Mum: But that will take ages!

Diane: Oh, all right. I 'll ring (ring) you when I get (get) there.

Helen: Don't forget to say hello to my friend Katrin, will you?

Diane: I won't forget. I 'll go (go) and see her as soon as I can.

Dad: Have you got enough money?

Diane: I hope so. I 'll tell (tell) you when there is (be) none left.

Simon: And don't come back too early.

Diane: Don't worry. I won't come (not come) back until I have (have) to.

d) *going to* oder *will*?

Diese beiden verwenden ***going to,*** weil es sich um eine Absicht handelt (vgl. S. 32).

Diese beiden verwenden ***will,*** weil es sich um einen spontanen Entschluß handelt (vgl. S. 34).

Diese beiden verwenden ***will,*** weil es sich um eine Vermutung handelt (vgl. S. 35).

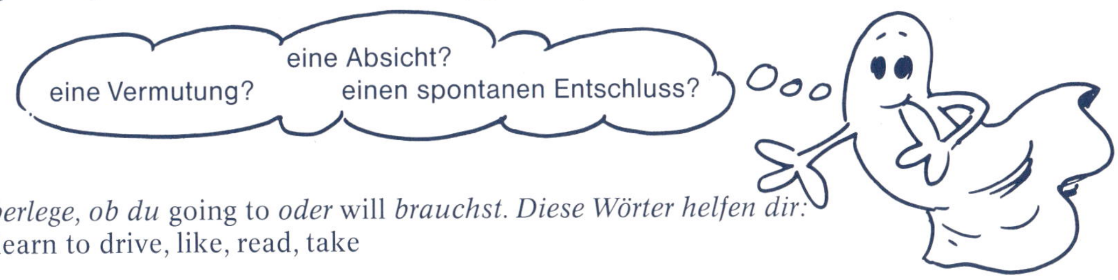

Was sagen diese Leute? Überlege, ob du going to *oder* will *brauchst. Diese Wörter helfen dir:*
answer, be late, be thirsty, learn to drive, like, read, take

12 *Present progressive* für die Zukunft

Die Verlaufsform der Gegenwart für die Zukunft

Das ***present progressive*** können wir sowohl für die Gegenwart als auch für die Zukunft gebrauchen.
Unterstreiche die **present progressive***-Formen in den folgenden Sätzen.*
Kreuze an, ob sie sich auf die Gegenwart oder auf die Zukunft beziehen.

	Gegenwart	Zukunft
You read a lot, don't you? – Yes, I'm reading "Moby Dick" at the moment. It's good.	☒	☐
Our friends are coming down from Hamburg this afternoon.	☐	☒
We're meeting them at the station.	☐	☒
I can't answer the phone. I'm washing my hair. Can you go?	☒	☐
Have you any holiday plans for next summer? – Yes, I'm visiting my penfriend in America.	☐	☒
Und hier? *"Whether you like it or not, we are dining with the Watsons."*	☐	☒

dine speisen

1. *Present progressive* für Vereinbarungen und feste Pläne

I can't come this afternoon. I**'m having** a driving lesson. (Der Termin steht fest.)
Dave**'s coming** tonight. (Wir haben uns verabredet.)
He**'s bringing** his new CDs. (Das haben wir ausgemacht.)

Wir verwenden das ***present progressive*** für die Zukunft, wenn etwas vereinbart oder fest geplant ist.

Wie würdest du diesen Beispielsatz ins Deutsche übersetzen?

I can't come this afternoon.
I'm having a driving lesson.

→ Ich kann heute Nachmittag nicht kommen. Ich habe eine Fahrstunde.

	Deutsch: Gegenwart	
Dave	**kommt**	heute Abend.
Dave	**is coming**	tonight.
	Englisch: *present progressive* (**nicht** *present simple*)	

Suche dir zwei dieser Veranstaltungen aus und schreibe zwei ähnliche Dialoge wie die obigen (zwei Leute verabreden sich). Die folgenden Wörter helfen dir:
the Vampires – play; the Starlight Disco – open; Johnny and Cass – sing; the Central Church – have

Lösungsbeispiele:

A: What are you doing on Wednesday afternoon? B: Nothing. Why?

A: Because the Starlight Disco is opening (at three o'clock). B: Great. Let's go (there).

A: Are you doing anything on Tuesday night?

B: Yes. I 'm going to the cinema with my dad. Why?

A: Because Johnny and Cass are singing at the Black Swan.

B: Sorry, I can't go on Tuesday.

A: What about Wednesday night?

B: All right. Let's go on Wednesday.

And you? *Welche Verabredungen und Termine hast du für die nächste Zeit? Schreibe Sätze wie diese:*
This afternoon/Next week/On Friday I'm meeting .../visiting .../playing ...
I'm ... tonight/next week/at the weekend. I'm not doing anything tomorrow/on Tuesday/......

2. *Present progressive* oder *going to*?

Du hast gelernt, dass man Zukunftspläne auch mit ***going to*** ausdrücken kann. Erkennst du den Bedeutungsunterschied zwischen ***present progressive*** und ***going to***?

Kreuze jeweils die richtige Ergänzung an:

Wenn wir etwas **beabsichtigen,** aber noch nicht fest geplant haben, verwenden wir
[x] ***going to.*** [ ] das ***present progressive.***

Wenn ein Plan so fest vereinbart ist, dass er kaum geändert werden kann, verwenden wir
[ ] ***going to.*** [x] das ***present progressive.***

Deshalb ist [ ] ***going to*** / [x] das ***present progressive*** besser für Ausreden, z. B.:

Welche Form gebrauchen diese Leute?
Entscheide zwischen going to *und* present progressive:

1. Shall we go swimming on Saturday afternoon?
   – I can't. I 'm taking (take) my little brother to the cinema.
2. Have you bought your train ticket yet?
   – No. I 'm going to buy (buy) it tomorrow.
3. Will you help me with my homework tonight?
   – Sorry, I 'm babysitting (babysit) for the neighbours.
4. Someone has stolen my bike! – What are you going to do (do)?
   – I 'm going to ring (ring) the police.

13 *If*-Sätze

Bedingungssätze

Durch Bedingungssätze kann man ausdrücken, was unter einer bestimmten Bedingung geschehen wird (1) oder geschehen würde (2):

(1)	***If*** you **go, I'll go** with you.	***Wenn*** du **gehst, gehe** ich mit.
(2)	**I'd go** with you ***if*** I **had** time.	Ich **würde mitgehen, *wenn*** ich Zeit **hätte**.

kein Komma!

Die Bedingung wird im Englischen meist durch einen Nebensatz mit *if* genannt.
Der *if*-Nebensatz kann vor oder nach dem Hauptsatz stehen.
Achtung: Im Englischen steht **vor *if* kein Komma.**

Sicher hast du schon bemerkt, dass die Bedingungssätze oben ganz unterschiedliche Bedeutungen haben und dass ganz unterschiedliche Verbformen benutzt werden.
Wir erklären dir jetzt die wichtigsten Typen von Bedingungssätzen.
Keine Angst, es ist nicht schwierig.

1. Erfüllbare oder realistische Bedingungen

If*-Nebensatz:** ***present simple	**Hauptsatz:** ***will-future***
If Bob **rings** up tonight,	**I'll ask** him to come over.
If Ken **doesn't hurry,**	he**'ll miss** the bus.
If he **misses** the bus,	he **won't be** in time for school.
If you **don't work** harder,	you **won't pass** the test.

(Zu den Formen von ***present simple*** und ***will-future*** vgl. S. 5, 7 und 34.)

Mit ***if***-Sätzen dieser Art drücken wir aus, was unter einer bestimmten Bedingung passieren wird. Wir halten diese Bedingung für realistisch: Es ist durchaus möglich, dass sie erfüllt wird.

Ergänze diese Sätze. Passende Ergänzungen stehen unten, aber in der falschen Reihenfolge. Außerdem musst du noch die richtigen Verbformen einsetzen:

1. If you give me your address, I'll write you a postcard.
2. I won't be able to play football tomorrow if my leg isn't better.
3. Ken will buy everyone an ice-cream if he passes his exam.
4. If we take the nine o'clock train, we'll arrive in London at twelve.
5. You'll get fat if you don't stop eating so many sweets.
6. If you give me some money, I'll do the shopping.
7. If Jean doesn't come to my party, I won't invite her again.
8. If you don't finish school, you'll be sorry one day.

you ... sorry one day (be)	if you ... eating so many sweets (not stop)
if my leg ... better (not be)	we ... in London at twelve (arrive)
I ... her again (not invite)	if he ... his exam (pass)
I ... you a postcard (write) ✓	I ... the shopping (do)

Bei den Zeitformen im Haupt- und Nebensatz darfst du dich nicht zu sehr vom Deutschen beinflussen lassen.
Vergleiche bitte:

Wenn du dich nicht **beeilst,**	**kommst** du zu spät.
If you **don't hurry,**	you**'ll be** late.

Im Deutschen benutzt man oft im Nebensatz **und** im Hauptsatz die Gegenwart/das Präsens.

Im Englischen darf man das ***present simple*** nur im Nebensatz benutzen.

Im Hauptsatz steht das will-future/die Zukunft mit will.

Übersetze bitte ins Englische:

1. Wenn du jetzt nicht ins Bett gehst, bist du morgen müde.
   If you don't go to bed now, you'll be tired tomorrow.
2. Ich helfe dir morgen, wenn du mir jetzt hilfst.
   I'll help you tomorrow if you help me now.
3. Wenn es am Wochenende schön ist, machen wir eine Fahrradtour.
   If is is fine/nice at the weekend, we'll go for a bike ride.
4. Wenn es morgen regnet, gehen wir ins Kino.
   If it rains tomorrow, we'll go to the cinema.

2. Unwahrscheinliche oder unrealistische Bedingungen

If*-Nebensatz:** ***past simple	**Hauptsatz:** ***would* + Grundform**
If I **saw** an UFO,	I**'d take** a photo of it.
If I **didn't take** a photo,	nobody **would believe** me.
If cars **ran** on water,	the air **wouldn't be** so polluted.
If there **weren't** any machines,	we **wouldn't have** so much free time.

(Zu den Formen des ***past simple*** vgl. S. 22/23. Die Kurzform von ***would*** ist ***'d.***)

Solche Bedingungssätze benutzen wir, wenn wir etwas für unwahrscheinlich oder gar unmöglich halten. Wir gehen von einer unrealistischen Bedingung aus und stellen uns nur vor, was wäre, wenn …

Achtung:
Kein ***would*** im ***if*-Nebensatz**

well-rested ausgeruht

Was könnten diese Leute besser machen? Ergänze die Sätze. Die Verben in Klammern helfen dir.

If Bob didn't go to bed so late,

he wouldn't be so tired every morning.

(not go, not be)

Linda's teeth wouldn't be so bad

if she didn't eat so many sweets.

(not be, not eat)

If Andy wrote a shopping list,

he wouldn't always forget

to buy something. (write, not forget)

If Barbara got a spare time job,

she would have some money.

(get, have)

If Diane's hair was/were shorter,

it would probably look better.

(be, look)

*What would **you** do in a situation like the following?*
*Wenn **dir** so etwas passieren würde wie diesen Leuten, würdest du dasselbe tun oder etwas anderes?*

1. Nick finds a wallet with a thousand pounds in a telephone box. He keeps it. Lösungsbeispiele:
   If I found a wallet with a thousand pounds,
   I'd take it to the police.

2. Sue feels lonely one afternoon. She rings up her aunt in Australia.
   If I felt lonely, I'd ring up/go and see a friend in my own town.

3. Pat misses the last bus home. She hitchhikes.

hitchhike per Anhalter fahren

If I missed the last bus home, I'd ring up my parents.

4. Bill is in Paris and loses his way. He goes to a police station.

If I was/were in Paris and lost my way, I'd look at/buy a map.

5. Tracy breaks her mother's favourite record. She tells her mother that her little brother broke it.

If I broke my mother's favourite record, I'd buy her a new one.

3. Nicht mehr erfüllbare Bedingungen

If*-Nebensatz:** ***past perfect	**Hauptsatz:** ***would have + past participle***
If we **had left** earlier,	we **wouldn't have missed** the bus.
If it **hadn't been** so rainy yesterday,	we **would have gone** to the beach.
(Wenn es gestern nicht so regnerisch **gewesen wäre,**	**wären** wir zum Strand **gegangen**.)

(Zu den Formen des ***past perfect*** vgl. S. 30. Zum ***past participle*** vgl. S. 15.)

Diese Art von Bedingungssätzen benutzen wir, wenn wir über die Vergangenheit sprechen. Die Bedingungen sind vollkommen unrealistisch, da sie sich nicht erfüllt haben und nicht mehr erfüllbar sind. Man stellt sich vor, was gewesen wäre, wenn …

Wenn es so und so gewesen wäre, dann … Aber in Wirklichkeit war es ja anders.
Schreibe unter die folgenden if-*Sätze, wie es wirklich war. Du brauchst dazu das* past simple.

1. If I had known that you were in hospital, I would have visited you.

I didn't know that you were in hospital. That's why I didn't visit you.

2. I would have helped you if I hadn't been so busy.

I didn't/couldn't help you because I was so/too busy.

3. We wouldn't have been late if there hadn't been so much traffic.

We were late because there was so much traffic.

4. If we had taken an umbrella, we wouldn't have got wet.

We didn't take an umbrella. That's why/So we got wet.

Mike is a very careless person.
Look what happened today,
for example.

He didn't lock his door.
His dog ran away.

He got up late.
So he missed the bus.

He didn't look where he was going.
A bike ran into him.

He put his glasses on a chair.
Someone sat on them.

He lost his girlfriend's telephone
number. He lost his girlfriend.

Now he is lying
in bed.
He thinks,
"What a day! . . ."

If I had locked my door,

my dog wouldn't have run away.

If I had got up earlier,

I wouldn't have missed the bus.

If I had looked where I was going,

the bike wouldn't have run into me.

If I hadn't put my glasses on that chair,

no one would have sat on them.

If I had written my girlfriend's number down,

I wouldn't have lost her.

14 Das Passiv

1. Aktiv und Passiv

Aktiv		Passiv	
The dog	**bit** the postman.	The postman	**was bitten** by the dog.
Der Hund	**biss** den Briefträger.	Der Briefträger	**wurde** vom Hund **gebissen**.

Der Aktivsatz und der Passivsatz beschreiben dieselbe Handlung, aber aus unterschiedlicher Sicht:

Im Aktivsatz geht es vor allem um den Hund :

Wir interessieren uns dafür, was er tat .

Im Passivsatz geht es vor allem um den Briefträger :

Wir interessieren uns dafür, was ihm passierte .

was ihm passierte?
Briefträger?
was er tat?
Hund?

2. Die Bildung des Passivs

Das Passiv kann in den meisten Zeitformen gebildet werden, z. B.

		Form von *be*	*past participle*	
present simple	I	am	*called*	Tiger by my friends.
	English	is	*spoken*	in many countries.
	Many cameras	are	*made*	in Japan.
past simple	The accident	was	*caused*	by a horse.
	Two people	were	*hurt.*	
present perfect simple	The world record	has not been	*broken*	yet.
	My clothes	have been	*stolen.*	
will-*future*	The road	will be	*opened*	next week.

Alles über das ***past participle*** findest du auf S. 15.

In Schlagzeilen der Presse und in Schilderaufschriften finden wir oft verkürzte Passivsätze. Weißt du, was diese hier bedeuten? Pass auf, dass du die richtige Zeitform wählst:
present simple *(3-mal)*, **present perfect simple** *(2-mal)*, **past simple** *(2-mal)*, ***will*-future** *(1-mal)*

Painting sold for two million

A painting has been sold for two million.

Five dogs stolen from dog's home

Five dogs have been stolen ______ from a dogs' home.

MISSING CHILDREN FOUND LAST NIGHT

The missing children were found last night.

New Sports Centre opened yesterday

The new sports centre was opened yesterday.

English is spoken here.

Dogs are not allowed in the park.

The library will be closed next Saturday.

Breakfast is served from 8.00 to 9.30.

3. Passivsätze ohne *by*

Aktiv: The paperboy **delivers** the paper at seven.

Passiv: The paper **is delivered** at seven.

This church **was built** in 1785.

My bike **has been stolen.**

Mum, the window **has been broken.**

Im Aktivsatz erfahren wir gleich zu Beginn, **wer** eine Handlung ausführt.
Im Passivsatz brauchen wir den ‚Täter' nicht zu nennen. Wir verwenden das Passiv deshalb z. B.,

- wenn es unwichtig ist, wer etwas tut oder getan hat,
- wenn wir es nicht wissen,
- wenn wir es verschleiern wollen.

In 1960 Barbara left the village of Twistledown in England to live in America. Now she has come back. She is talking about the changes in the village:
Verwende Passivformen der Verben in Klammern, um Barbaras Bericht zu vervollständigen.

"It's not the same. A lot of new houses have been built (build). Some big old houses have been changed (change) into flats. The school has been modernized (modernize). A lot of new shops have been opened (open). The cinema has been closed (close). A new road has been built (build). I don't like it so much any more."

Today Stella's class is visiting a large international hotel, Hotel Europe.
The pupils talk to some of the people who work there.

Nach dem Besuch soll die Klasse einen Bericht über einen typischen Tagesablauf im Hotel Europe schreiben.
Kannst du Stella bei ihrem Bericht helfen?
Dazu musst du die Reihenfolge der abgebildeten Handlungen etwas verändern.

The newspapers are delivered at 7.00. They are put on the tables in the hall.

Breakfast is served from 7.30 to 9.00. Then the tables are cleared and laid for lunch. Fresh flowers are put on the tables.

The rooms are cleaned from 10.00 to 12.00: the beds are made and the wastepaper baskets are emptied. The dirty washing is put into baskets. It is collected by a van at 12.30.

Lunch is served from 12.30 to 2. Then the tables are cleared and laid for dinner.

The letters are taken to the post office at 3.

4. Passivsätze mit *by*

The new disco **will be opened *by Princess Di.***
America **was discovered *by Christopher Columbus.***

The accident **was caused *by a horse.***
The church **has been destroyed *by fire.***

Wenn wir betonen wollen, **wer** eine Handlung ausführt oder ausgeführt hat, benutzen wir Passivsätze mit ***by***.

Dies gilt auch, wenn die Handlung nicht durch einen Menschen verursacht wurde.

Findest du heraus, wer was gemacht hat?

The Parthenon was built by the Greeks. (build)

'Yesterday' was sung by the Beatles. (sing)

The first Mickey Mouse films were made by Walt Disney. (make)

The first walkmen were sold by Sony. (sell)

The Mona Lisa was painted by Leonardo da Vinci. (paint)

The car industry was started by Henry Ford. (start)

Sony
the Beatles
the Greeks
Leonardo da Vinci
Henry Ford
Walt Disney

Have a laugh!

Teacher: Can you tell me where elephants are found?
Girl: Elephants are so big, they're hardly ever lost.

Fred was very angry when he was asked to take off his mask at a party.
– Why?
– He wasn't wearing one.

Why are you standing in that bowl of water?
– Well, these tablets have to be taken in water three times a day.

bowl [bəʊl] Schüssel

15 Hilfsverben wie *can, may, must* usw.

1. Besonderheiten der Hilfsverben wie *can, may, must* usw.

Die englischen Hilfsverben ***can, may, must, need, shall, will*** unterscheiden sich in vielen Punkten von ‚normalen' Verben wie ***go, like, think*** usw. (Vollverben). Sie unterscheiden sich auch von den entsprechenden deutschen Verben ***können, dürfen, müssen*** usw.

I **must go** to school now. Vgl.: Ich **muss** jetzt zur Schule **(gehen).**	Sie können nur zusammen mit der Grundform eines Vollverbs verwendet werden.
She **can speak** French. Vgl.: She **speaks** French.	Sie haben kein ***-s*** in der 3. Person Einzahl im ***present simple.***
Can you **play** the guitar? Vgl.: **Do** you **play** the guitar?	In Fragen mit diesen Hilfsverben wird nie das Hilfsverb ***do*** benützt (vgl. S. 59 und 61).
He **needn't help** me. Vgl.: He **doesn't help** me.	Dasselbe gilt für die Verneinung.
You **must** get up now. (Du **musst** jetzt aufstehen.) We **had to** get up very early this morning. (Wir **mussten** heute Morgen sehr früh aufstehen.) **Can** we go out? (**Dürfen/Können** wir hinausgehen?) We **weren't allowed to** leave the room. (Wir **durften** den Raum nicht verlassen.)	Von den deutschen Verben ***können, müssen*** usw. kann man alle Zeitformen bilden. Bei den englischen Hilfsverben ist dies nicht möglich. Deshalb muss man oft ein Vollverb mit ähnlicher Bedeutung benützen, z. B. ***have to*** für ***müssen*** und ***be allowed to*** für ***dürfen.***

Wie gut kannst du schon mit den englischen Hilfsverben umgehen? Übersetze diese Sätze ins Englische. Du musst dabei manchmal ein Verb benutzen, wo im deutschen Satz gar keines steht, z. B.:

go, leave, speak, walk

1. Es ist spät. Ich muss jetzt weg.

   It's late. I must/have to go/leave now.

2. Ben hat gestern den Bus verpasst. Er musste zu Fuß nach Hause.

   Ben missed the bus yesterday. He had to walk home.

3. Mein Brieffreund kann sehr gut Deutsch.

   My pen-friend can speak German very well.

4. Darf ich deinen Brief lesen?

   Can/May I read your letter?

5. Ich war letzte Woche krank und durfte nicht aus dem Haus.

   I was ill last week and wasn't allowed to leave the house.

*"What **I** wear, Mrs Preston, is not the problem. But as a pupil your son **must** wear a school uniform!"*

2. *Can, can't, could, couldn't*

a) Für Fähigkeiten und Möglichkeiten

Horses **can** sleep standing up.
Cats **can't** swim.
It has stopped raining. We **can** go out now.
You **cannot** buy anything today. The shops are closed.
Steffi **could** play tennis when she was five.
We **couldn't** watch the match last night, because our TV broke down.

Mit ***can*** kann man Fähigkeiten und Möglichkeiten beschreiben.

⚠ Beachte die Schreibung von ***cannot!***

Mit der Vergangenheitsform ***could*** kann man über vergangene Fähigkeiten und Möglichkeiten sprechen.

I can't find my mouth.

Beschreibe, was bestimmte Tiere können oder nicht können. Du kannst die Stichwörter im Kasten verwenden oder dir selbst etwas ausdenken.

camels	elephants	fly	swim	run very fast	
penguins	fish	hear/see very well		jump	
ducks	monkeys ...	use tools		live without water	...

Lösungsbeispiele:
Camels can live without water for a long time.

Penguins can't fly. Ducks can swim. Fish can't live without water.

Monkeys can use tools. Elephants can't jump.

Dogs can't see very well. Horses can run very fast.

Cats can't swim. Cats can see in the dark.

Budgies can learn to speak.

Have you ever broken your arm? Wendy broke hers six months ago. There were so many things she couldn't do without help.

Which of these things do you think she ***could*** *or* ***couldn't*** *do without help?*

eat with a spoon, eat with a knife and fork, wash her hands, wash her hair, open tins, open bottles, play the guitar, play volleyball, put her anorak on, ride a bike, take her dog for a walk, use her computer

Lösungsbeispiele:
She could eat with a spoon. She couldn't eat with a knife and fork.

She couldn't wash her hands. She couldn't wash her hair.

She couldn't open tins. She could open bottles.

She couldn't play the guitar. She couldn't play volleyball.

She couldn't put her anorak on. She couldn't ride a bike.

She could take her dog for a walk.

She could use her computer.

Can you think of any other things she could or couldn't do?

Lösungsbeispiele:
She could write. She couldn't play cards. She couldn't go swimming.

She could read books and comics.

She could use the telephone.

b) Für Bitten, Erlaubnis/Verbot, Angebote, Vorschläge

Can/Could you tell me the time, please? **Can/Could** you show me your passport, please? **Can/Could** I use your telephone, please? – Yes, of course you **can**.	Mit ***can*** oder ***could*** können wir jemand um einen Gefallen oder um Erlaubnis bitten. ***Could*** wirkt noch höflicher als ***can.***
Can I go to the pop concert? – No, you **can't**.	Mit ***can*** und ***can't*** können wir etwas erlauben oder verbieten.
Can I help you? – I'm looking for Mr Brown. – I **can** take you to his office.	Mit ***can*** können wir anbieten, etwas für jemand zu tun.
We **could** go for a bike ride this afternoon.	Mit ***could*** können wir einen Vorschlag machen.

Übersetze diese beiden Sätze:

1. **Could** you say that again, please? Könntest du/Könnten Sie das bitte wiederholen?
2. **Could** you understand the people when you were in Ireland? Konntest du die Leute verstehen, als du in Irland warst?

Was fällt dir auf?

In Satz 2 wird ***could*** als **Vergangenheitsform** benutzt, in Satz 1 als **Möglichkeitsform.**

Was sagen diese Leute?
Benutze can, could, can't *und folgende Ausdrücke:*

show me your licence · carry something · help me · go to the cinema · play ball here · repeat it · use mine

3. *Must, mustn't, needn't* und *have to*

a) *Must* und *have to* für eine Notwendigkeit

I always **have to** be home by eleven. – You're lucky.
I**'ve got to** be home by ten.
When **do** you **have to** get up? – At seven, usually.

I **had to** go to the dentist's yesterday.
My sister is ill. We **have had to** fetch the doctor.

Mit ***I must*** drücken wir aus, dass wir uns etwas dringend vornehmen.
Mit ***you must*** fordern wir jemand auf, etwas zu tun, das heißt, wir üben Zwang auf jemand aus.

Wenn man nur sachlich über eine Notwendigkeit spricht, also selbst keinen Zwang ausüben will, benutzt man im ***present simple*** meistens ***have to*** oder ***have got to.***
In anderen Zeitformen kann man nur ***have to*** verwenden (z. B. ***had to*** im ***past simple***).

Aufgepasst bei *müssen:*
Gehe sparsam mit ***must*** um, sonst kannst du leicht den Eindruck erwecken, dass du die Leute herumkommandieren willst.
Have (got) to ist meistens eher angebracht.

"I really must get myself a pair of steps."

a pair of steps Trittleiter

What are these people saying? *Benutze* must:

Who has to do what?
Was ist für diese Berufe typisch?
Bilde Sätze mit have to:

fireman	go out in all weathers
waiter	get up very early
baker	be ready to help at all times
sportsman	be friendly to all customers
taxi driver	know the town very well
postwoman	train a lot

A fireman has to be ready to help at all times.

A waiter has to be friendly to all customers.

A baker has to get up very early.

A sportsman has to train a lot.

A taxi driver has to know the town very well.

A postwoman has to go out in all weathers.

What did they have to do? *Kannst du die Sätze ergänzen?*

1. Yesterday I missed the last bus, so I had to walk all the way home.
2. Pete's party was great. Why did you leave so early? – I had to be home by ten.
3. Was entrance to the museum free? – No, we had to pay 50p each.
4. Before there were washing machines people had to wash all their clothes by hand.

Mit must *kann man auch logische Schlussfolgerungen ausdrücken (wie mit* müssen *im Deutschen):*

1. Mary is ten. She is four years younger than Paul. So Paul must be fourteen.
2. A doctor from Boston has a brother who is a sailor. The sailor has no brother.

   So the doctor must be the sailor's sister.

Kannst du ein ähnliches Rätsel schreiben?

Lösungsbeispiel:

A taxi driver from London has a daughter who is a nurse. The nurse's father died five years ago.

So the taxi driver must be the nurse's mother.

b) *Must, mustn't, needn't* und *don't/doesn't/didn't have to*

You **must** stay in bed.

You **mustn't** get up.
(Du darfst nicht aufstehen.)

You **needn't** wait for me. I'll be late tonight.
(Du **brauchst nicht** auf mich zu warten./Du **musst nicht** auf mich warten.)

I **haven't got to/don't have to** wash up today. It's my sister's turn.
My uncle grows his own vegetables. He **doesn't have/need to** buy any.

Our flight to Chicago was non-stop. We **didn't have/need to** change planes.
It's getting warmer. Next month we **won't have/need to** heat the flat any more.

Mit ***you must*** fordert man jemand auf, etwas **zu tun.**

Mit ***you mustn't*** fordert man jemand auf, etwas **zu unterlassen,** das heißt, man verbietet etwas.

Mit ***you needn't*** erklärt man etwas für nicht nötig.

Um zu sagen, dass etwas nicht nötig ist, sagt man auch ***haven't/hasn't got to, don't/doesn't have to*** oder ***don't/doesn't need to.***

In anderen Zeitformen als ***present simple*** kann man nur eine verneinte Form von ***have to*** oder ***need to*** benutzen, also z. B. ***didn't have to*** oder ***didn't need to*** im ***past simple.***

"You boy, write out sixty times 'I must not be a vandal.'"

vandal [ˈvændl] jemand, der Sachen mutwillig beschädigt

You **must** turn right.
(Du **musst** . . .)

You **mustn't** turn right.
(Du **darfst nicht** . . .)

You **needn't** turn right.
(Du **musst nicht/brauchst nicht** . . .)

FARAWAY TRAVEL AGENCY

is looking for bright and friendly young people.

Good English important. Should speak German.
French useful, but not essential.
Experience not necessary. We'll train you.
Interesting work. No overtime. Canteen.

essential [ɪˈsenʃl]/
necessary [ˈnesəsrɪ]
notwendig
(work) overtime
Überstunden
(machen)
canteen Kantine

WANT A HOLIDAY JOB?

Are you aged 18–30?
Do you live in or near Manchester?
We're on the main bus route.
We work Mon.–Fri. 9–5

Come and see us. Or ring 006756.

Must, mustn't *oder* needn't? *Entscheide dich für die passende Form:*

For the job at the travel agency you must be bright and friendly. You mustn't be bad at English. You needn't speak French. You needn't have experience. You needn't work overtime and you needn't bring your own food.

For the holiday job you must be 18 or more, but you mustn't be older than 30. You mustn't live a long way from Manchester. You needn't have a car. You needn't work on Saturdays. And you needn't go there, you can ring them.

Der kleine Tim findet, dass die Kinder es in der Steinzeit besser hatten, weil sie bestimmte Dinge, die er hasst, nicht zu tun brauchten. Kannst du die einzelnen Gründe für ihn aufschreiben?

Children in the Stone Age
didn't have to wash their faces.

They didn't have to make their beds.

They didn't have to clean their shoes.

They didn't have to go to school.

They didn't have to do (any) homework.

4. *May* und *might*

I haven't seen Mike for days. He **may *be*** ill.
(Er ***ist* vielleicht** krank.)

Could you talk to Sue tomorrow? – I **may not *see*** her. (Ich ***sehe*** sie **vielleicht nicht**.)

Take your umbrella. It **might** rain today.
I **might** go to England next summer. But I don't know yet. I **might not** have enough money.

May I ask you to follow me?

Mit ***may*** können wir Vermutungen äußern. Es entspricht etwa dem deutschen ***vielleicht***.

May not entspricht etwa dem deutschen ***vielleicht nicht***.

Statt ***may (not)*** können wir auch ***might (not)*** benutzen. Der Bedeutungsunterschied ist gering. ***Might (not)*** drückt etwas größeren Zweifel aus.

Mit ***may*** können wir im förmlichen Stil auch um Erlaubnis bitten. In der Umgangssprache ist jedoch ***can*** üblich (vgl. S. 52).

Kannst du die unterstrichenen Sätze durch Sätze mit may *oder* might *ersetzen?*

I'm leaving.
Perhaps I won't come back. — I may not come back.

Uncle Mel hasn't come to see us for ages. Maybe he'll come tonight. — He may/might come tonight.

I'm afraid of the exam.
Perhaps I won't pass it. — I may/might not pass it.

My walkman doesn't work any more.
Maybe the batteries are empty. — The batteries may/might be empty.

Stop that music.
Perhaps the neighbours don't like it. — The neighbours may/might not like it.

What about you? What might happen?
Denke dir ein paar Sätze aus:

This afternoon ______

This evening ______

At the weekend ______

Next summer ______

When I leave school ______

In twenty years' time ______

'Can you think of anyone who might have a grudge against you?'

traffic warden Verkehrskontrolleur, der die Einhaltung von Parkvorschriften überwacht – **grudge** Groll, Hass

5. *Shall* und *should*

Shall I help you?
Where **shall** we put our coats?
Shall we have a picnic on Sunday?

We **should** keep the countryside clean.
People **shouldn't** throw cans and bottles into rivers.

Shall kommt praktisch nur in Fragen vor. Mit ***shall I/ shall we*** fragen wir, was wir tun sollen. Mit ***shall we*** können wir auch einen Vorschlag machen.

Should und ***shouldn't*** benutzen wir, um zu raten, warnen oder tadeln.

Was sollte man tun oder nicht tun, um unsere Umwelt zu erhalten?
Du kannst die Stichwörter im Kasten benutzen, aber sicher hast du auch eigene Ideen.

We/You/People should/shouldn't ...
try to save energy — go everywhere by car
use buses or trains if possible — drive as fast as possible
throw away empty bottles — recycle used things
use a lot of washing powder — have baths — have showers

Lösungsbeispiele:

People should try to save energy. We shouldn't go everywhere by car.

We should use buses or trains if possible.

People shouldn't drive as fast as possible.

We shouldn't throw away empty bottles.

We should recycle (used) things.

People shouldn't use a lot of washing powder.

We shouldn't have many baths.

We should have showers instead.

People should plant more trees.

'It says here we should beware of local pickpockets.'

space guide Weltraumführer – **beware of** sich in Acht nehmen vor – **pickpocket** Taschendieb

What should or shouldn't these people do?

They shouldn't leave the car.

She shouldn't touch the painting/picture.

They should ask the/a policeman.

She should put on her jacket.

He shouldn't climb the (old) oak/tree.

6. *Will, would, would like* und *want to*

I don't know the way to Cardiff. – **I'll** bring you a map tomorrow.
Will/Would you open the window, please? (Würdest du bitte das Fenster öffnen?)

Will benutzt man oft, um über die Zukunft zu sprechen (vgl. S. 34).
Mit *will* oder *would* können wir jemand um einen Gefallen bitten. *Would* wirkt höflicher.

Sue **doesn't want to** stay at school. She **wants to** get a job. (Sue **will nicht** auf der Schule bleiben. Sie **will** sich eine Stelle suchen.)
What **do** you **want to** be? (Was **willst** du einmal werden?)
Bill **wanted to** be a doctor, but he didn't pass his exam. (Bill **wollte** Arzt werden, ...)

⚠ Das deutsche Verb *wollen* kann praktisch nie mit *will* oder *would* übersetzt werden. Meistens müssen wir *want to* benutzen.

Would you **like to** come out with me on Saturday? (**Möchtest** du/**Würdest** du **gerne** ... ?)
Mr Miller **would like to** speak to you.
I'd like to talk to the manager, please.

Want to kann manchmal ziemlich grob klingen (genauso wie *wollen* im Deutschen). Um einen Wunsch höflicher zu äußern oder zu erfragen, benutzen wir *would like to.*

Übersetze die folgenden Sätze ins Englische:

1. Ich will im Sommer in Urlaub fahren. Ich will nicht zu Hause bleiben.

   I want to go on holiday this summer. I don't want to stay at home.

2. Würdest du bitte auf mich warten? Would you wait for me, please?

3. Warum hast du gestern Abend deine Schwester nicht mitgebracht? – Sie wollte nicht kommen.

   Why didn't you bring your sister last night? – She didn't want to come.

'Please, sir, I'd like to be a barber.'

barber Herrenfriseur

'If she doesn't make it as a ballet dancer, she wants to be a dentist.'

make it es schaffen

What would or wouldn't **you** like to do when you're older?
Du kannst bei deiner Antwort z. B. folgende Verben benutzen: work, live, travel, meet, see, earn

I'd like to

16 Fragesätze

1. Entscheidungsfragen (Fragen ohne Fragewort)

snail Schnecke
anybody *hier:* jeden

a) Das Hilfsverb in Entscheidungsfragen

Aussagesatz				**Fragesatz**			
S	H			H	S		
Ann	**has**	**gone**	out.	**Has**	Ann	**gone**	out?
They	**have**	**got**	a dog.	**Have**	they	**got**	a dog?
Pete	**will**	**come**	back.	**Will**	Pete	**come**	back?
Steve	**is**	**reading.**		**Is**	Steve	**reading?**	
We		**are**	ready.	**Are**	we		ready?
Bill		**was**	ill.	**Was**	Bill		ill?
Pam		**goes**	jogging.	**Does**	Pam	**go**	jogging?
You		**play**	tennis.	**Do**	you	**play**	tennis?
Ken		**climbed**	Ben Nevis.	**Did**	Ken	**climb**	Ben Nevis?

Wenn im Aussagesatz ein **Hilfsverb** (H) oder eine Form des Verbs ***be*** vorhanden ist, musst du das Hilfsverb oder die Form von ***be*** vor das **Subjekt** (S) stellen.
Wenn weder ein Hilfsverb noch eine Form von ***be*** vorhanden ist, musst du das Hilfsverb ***do*** verwenden. (Vgl. S. 7 und 23.)

Achtung: Anders als im Deutschen darfst du im Englischen eine Frage nie mit einem Vollverb wie ***play, like, love*** usw. beginnen.

Vergleiche:

Do you **love** me? (Tust du mich lieben?) — **Liebst** du mich?

Auch ***have*** und das Verb ***do*** selbst können als Vollverben vorkommen.
Wenn kein anderes Hilfsverb vorhanden ist, musst du in der Frage ***do*** als Hilfsverb benutzen.

Aussagesatz:		**Fragesatz:**
The town **has got** a swimming-pool.		**Has** the town **got** a swimming-pool?
You **had** a nice day.	**Aber:**	Did you have a nice day?
Sue **has** eggs for breakfast.		Does Sue have eggs for breakfast ?
Linda **has done** her job.		Has Linda done her job ?
Sam **does** his homework in the kitchen.	**Aber:**	Does Sam do his homework in the kitchen?
Linda **did** the job well.		Did Linda do the job well ?

Sabine has a new penfriend and wants to know lots of things about her.
Ergänze Sabines Fragen durch das passende Hilfsverb:

Have you got any brothers or sisters?

Do you live in a house or flat?

Are you interested in tennis?

Did you watch Steffi Graf play last week?

Does your school have a football team?

Have you ever been to Germany?

Do you want to come and see me?

*Welche Fragen würdest **du** deinem Brieffreund oder deiner Brieffreundin stellen?*
Lösungsbeispiele:

Are you interested in sports? Do you do any sports?

Do you read a lot? Do you like comics?

Have you got any pets? Can you play an instrument?

b) Entscheidungsfragen und Kurzantworten

Frage				Kurzanwort		
H	S				S	H
Does	Jane	**like**	chips?	Yes,	she	**does.**
				No,	she	**doesn't.**
Has	the taxi	**arrived?**		Yes,	it	**has.**
				No,	it	**hasn't.**
Can	the boys	**go?**		Yes,	they	**can.**
				No,	they	**can't.**
Are	you	hungry?		Yes,	I	**am.**
				No,	I	**'m not.**

Entscheidungsfragen werden im Englischen selten nur mit ***yes*** oder ***no*** beantwortet. Dies wird als zu schroff empfunden. Meist weitet man ***yes*** oder ***no*** zu einer Kurzantwort aus:
Man nimmt das Subjekt und das Hilfsverb der Frage wieder auf.

Ist das Subjekt der Frage ein Hauptwort wie ***my friend, Jane, the train, the boys,*** benutzt man in der Kurzantwort ***he, she, it*** oder ***they.***

Bei ***No*** benutzt man ein verneintes Hilfsverb.

Kannst du diese Fragen beantworten?
Benutze Kurzantworten.

A QUIZ

Did Robin Hood live in London?	No, he didn't.
Is Glasgow an English city?	No, it isn't.
Has Canada got any big cities?	Yes, it has.
Do all Canadians speak English?	No, they don't.
Was Alfred Hitchcock British?	Yes, he was.
Was Captain Cook an Australian?	No, he wasn't.
Do kangaroos eat other animals?	No, they don't.
Are dolphins fish?	No, they aren't.
Can crocodiles run?	Yes, they can.

Kannst du dein eigenes Quiz entwerfen? Schreibe ein paar Entscheidungsfragen auf und lasse die Kurzantworten von einem Mitschüler oder einer Mitschülerin ausfüllen.
Lösungsbeispiele:

Is Cardiff in England?	No, it isn't.
Is Canada larger than the USA?	Yes, it is.
Do the Americans drive on the left?	No, they don't.
Do the Australians drive on the left?	Yes, they do.

2. Bestimmungsfragen (Fragen mit Fragewort)

a) Fragen mit Fragewort + Hilfsverb + Subjekt

Bestimmungsfragen beginnen mit einem Fragewort (F). Ansonsten werden die meisten Bestimmungsfragen wie Entscheidungsfragen gebildet.
(Vgl. S. 59. Ausnahmen S. 62.)

Aussagesatz				**Fragesatz**			
S	H			F	H	S	
John	**has**	**gone**	out.	***Where***	**has**	he	**gone?**
Kay	**can't**	**come**	to the party.	***Why***	**can't**	she	**come?**
She		**is**	on holiday.	***Where***	**is**	she?	
I		**read**	a lot.	***What***	**do**	you	**read?**
Bob		**knows**	our secret.	***How***	**does**	he	**know?**
Sue		**phoned**	yesterday.	***When***	**did**	she	**phone?**

Ist ein Hilfsverb (H) oder eine Form von ***be*** vorhanden, so werden diese vor das Subjekt (S) gestellt. Ist weder ein Hilfsverb noch eine Form von ***be*** vorhanden, so wird das Hilfsverb ***do*** verwendet.

Jimmy is talking to Helen at the youth club.
He is new here.
What does he ask Helen?

Ergänze Jimmys Fragen.
Du musst dabei das present simple *der Verben in Klammern verwenden.*

Jim:		**Helen:**
Where do you live ?	(live)	In a village about fifteen miles from here.
How do you get here?	(get)	By motor-bike.
How often do you come ?	(come)	About three times a week.
When does the club open ?	(the club/open)	On Tuesdays, Fridays and Sundays.
What time does it open on Sundays?	(it/open)	At two.
And when does it close ?	(it/close)	At half past nine.

Somebody broke into the Graysons' house when they were out last night.
What questions does the police inspector ask?
Benutze folgende Verben:
arrive, get in, go, take, be

burglar [ˈbɜːglə] Einbrecher

Where did you go last night?

When did you arrive home?

How long were you out?

How did the burglars get in ?

What did they take ?

Where was your money?

b) Fragen nach dem Subjekt

Im Englischen spielt die Wortstellung für die Bedeutung von Fragen eine große Rolle. Dies zeigt das Beispiel rechts.

***Who* can see** Carol? – Mary.
Wer sieht Carol?

***Who* can** Carol **see?** – Steve.
Wen sieht Carol?

Wir fragen nach dem Subjekt (S)				Wir fragen nach etwas anderem			
S/F	H			F	H	S	
Kim	**has**	**invited**	Paul.				
Who	**has**	**invited**	Paul? – Kim.	***Who***	**has**	Kim	**invited?** – Paul.
Ann		**kissed**	Tony.				
Who		**kissed**	Tony? – Ann.	***Who***	**did**	Ann	**kiss?** – Tony.
Which of you		**knows** Ken Wood? – I do.		***Which of you***	**does**	Ken	**know?** – None of us.
What		**damaged** the house? – A storm.		***What***	**did** the storm		**damage?** – A house.
Wenn wir nach dem Subjekt fragen ***(wer, was*** oder ***welcher)***, ist die Wortstellung wie im Aussagesatz. Das Subjekt wird einfach durch ein Fragewort (z. B. ***who, which, what***) ersetzt. Das Hilfsverb ***do*** wird **nicht** benutzt.				Wenn wir nach jemand oder etwas anderem als dem Subjekt fragen, wird das Hilfsverb zwischen Fragewort und Subjekt gestellt. Ist kein Hilfsverb vorhanden, so **muss** das Hilfsverb ***do*** benutzt werden.			

Kannst du die Fragen zu diesem Kreuzworträtsel stellen? Wandle die folgenden Sätze in Fragen mit who *oder* what *um:*

1. It grows on your head.
2. You can eat it. (It is also a colour.)
3. He flew from New York to Paris in 1927.
4. Columbus met them when he landed in America.
5. He or she plays records.
6. You call them Aussies.
7. It has 12 months.
8. It comes after winter.
9. Most pupils love them.

O.K., I give up – WHAT has twenty legs and barks?

H	A	I	R							
O	R	A	N	G	E					
L	I	N	D	B	E	R	G	H		
I	N	D	I	A	N	S				
D	I	S	C		J	O	C	K	E	Y
A	U	S	T	R	A	L	I	A	N	S
Y	E	A	R							
S	P	R	I	N	G					

1. What grows on your head?
2. What can you eat (and is also a colour)?
3. Who flew from New York to Paris in 1927?
4. Who did Columbus meet when he landed in America?
5. Who plays records?
6. Who do you call Aussies?
7. What has 12 months?
8. What comes after winter?
9. What do most pupils love?

17 Der Infinitiv

Die Grundform des Verbs

I've forgotten **to buy** new batteries.
We've decided ***not* to go** on holiday this year.

I ***must* buy** new batteries for my calculator.
Please, ***let*** me **go**.

Der Infinitiv kommt im Satz meistens mit ***to*** vor.
Zur Verneinung stellt man ***not*** davor.

Nur nach Hilfsverben wie ***can, may, must*** usw. (vgl. S. 50) und nach wenigen Vollverben steht der Infinitiv ohne ***to***.

Achte darauf, ob das Verb vor dem Infinitiv verneint ist oder der Infinitiv selbst. Der Bedeutungsunterschied kann sehr groß sein. Übersetze die folgenden Sätze ins Deutsche:

Try not to break the bottle.

Versuche, die Flasche nicht zu zerbrechen.

Don't try to break the bottle.

Versuche nicht, die Flasche zu zerbrechen.

"... and try not to lope."

lope
in großen Sätzen springen

1. Der Infinitiv mit *to* nach bestimmten Verben

I'***d like* to go** to Britain one day.
***Try* not to come** late next time.
What ***do*** you ***want* to do** when you leave school?
Would you ***like* to come** to the youth club? –
I'***d love* to.** (= I'd love to come.)

Der Infinitiv mit ***to*** steht vor allem nach Verben, die Wünsche, Absichten und Ziele ausdrücken, z. B. ***want, would like, plan, try.***
Um Wiederholungen zu vermeiden, kann man nur ***to*** statt ***to*** + Infinitiv verwenden.

Merke dir vor allem folgende Verben mit ***to*** + Infinitiv:	decide expect forget	hope learn plan	promise try want	would like would love would prefer

Warum tun diese Leute etwas Bestimmtes? Wähle die passenden Verben und Stichwörter aus:

do her homework	has forgotten	is learning ✓	speak French ✓
go there on holiday	has promised	meet her mother at five	wants

Steve has bought these cassettes because he is learning to speak French.

Jane is reading a book about Spain because she wants to go there on holiday.

Wendy is looking at her watch because she has promised to meet her mother at five.

The teacher is angry because Ann has forgotten to do her homework.

2. Verben mit Objekt und Infinitiv

	Verb	Obj.	Infinitiv
I	***'ll ask***	***Tony***	**to help** me.
The headmaster	***told***	***us***	**to wait** outside.
My parents	***don't allow***	***me***	**to stay** out late.

Nach den meisten Verben, die eine Aufforderung oder Erlaubnis ausdrücken, steht ein Objekt (die Person, die etwas tun soll oder darf) und der Infinitiv mit ***to***.

The police ***warn drivers*** **to lock** their cars.

The police ***warn drivers not*** **to leave** their car doors open.

⚠ ***warn someone to do something***
= jemand ermahnen, etwas zu tun
warn s.o. not to do s.th.
= jd. ermahnen, etwas **nicht** zu tun;
jd. davor warnen, etwas zu tun

Aunt Liz ***wants us*** **to meet** her at the station.
(Tante Liz will, dass wir sie ... abholen.)
Would you ***like me*** **to come** with you?
(Möchtest du, dass ich mitkomme?)
Harry ***expects me*** **to write** him a postcard.
(Harry erwartet, dass ich ihm ... schreibe.)

Auch nach ***want, would like*** und ***expect*** steht ein Objekt mit Infinitiv, wenn jemand will, dass **ein anderer** etwas tut.

⚠ Im Deutschen benutzt man hier einen Dass-Satz. Im Englischen darf nach ***want*** und ***would like*** kein ***that***-Satz stehen.

The people who put up these notices want you to do some things, but they don't want you to do others. Can you say what?

Benutze die Verben in Klammern. Pass auf! Manchmal musst du den Infinitiv verneinen.

"Waiter, why have you got your finger on my steak?"
"I don't want it to fall on the floor again, sir."

NO PARKING — They don't allow you to park here.
(not allow)

Please do not feed the animals. — They ask you not to feed the animals.
(ask)

NO FOOD, PLEASE. — They don't want you to take/eat any food in here.
(not want)

They tell you not to pick (any) flowers.
(tell)

DANGER! Drive slowly. — They warn you to drive slowly.
(warn)

They warn you not to drink and drive.
(warn)

let someone do something: **zulassen/erlauben, dass jemand etwas tut**	***make someone do something:*** **veranlassen/erzwingen, dass jemand etwas tut**
The guard ***let the prisoner*** **escape.** (Der Wachposten ließ den Gefangenen entkommen.)	The captain ***made the sailors*** **work** hard all day. (... ließ die Matrosen ... hart arbeiten.)

Das deutsche Verb ***lassen*** ist doppeldeutig. Im Englischen unterscheidet man zwischen „zulassen" = ***let*** und „veranlassen" = ***make.*** Nach ***let*** + Objekt und ***make*** + Objekt steht der Infinitiv **ohne *to***.

Ergänze diese Witze, damit du sie anderen erzählen kannst. Entscheide zwischen make *und* let. *Außerdem brauchst du folgende Verben:* bring, grow, pay, sit (2 x)

1. What happened to the boy who ran away with the circus?

   – The police ___made___ him ___bring___ it back.

2. Mum, shall I ___let___ my hair ___grow___ ?

   – I don't think you can stop it.

3. I went to see a psychiatrist about my bad memory.

   – What did he do?

   – He ___made___ me ___pay___ in advance.

psychiatrist [saɪˈkaɪətrɪst] Psychiater – **memory** Gedächtnis – **in advance** im Voraus

'It's part of the punishment. Stripes make us look fat.'

stripes Streifen

4. A very fat lady was sitting on the bus. Three old ladies were standing. She said to the man next to her, "If you were a gentleman,

   you'd get up and ___let___ one of these ladies ___sit___ down."

   He answered, "If you were a lady, you'd get up and ___let___ all three ___sit___ down."

*What do **your** parents make or let you do?*
*What **don't** they make or let you do?*
Here are some ideas:

My father/mother/parents – watch TV until ...
wear lipstick – work in the garden – go to bed at ...

____

____

____

3. Der Infinitiv mit *to* zum Ausdruck eines Zwecks und nach Adjektiven (Eigenschaftswörtern)

Linda is looking for a part-time job **to earn** money for a trip to France. (..., um Geld für eine Reise nach Frankreich zu verdienen.)

Durch den Infinitiv mit ***to*** kannst du sagen, zu welchem Zweck etwas geschieht (wie im Deutschen durch den Infinitiv mit ***um zu***).

Bob is ***too*** young **to drive** a car, but he's old ***enough*** **to ride** a moped. (Bob ist zu jung, um ein Auto zu fahren, aber er ist alt genug, um ein Moped zu fahren.)

Auch nach Ausdrücken mit ***too*** und ***enough*** kannst du den Infinitiv verwenden (um zu sagen, für welchen Zweck jemand z. B. zu jung oder alt genug ist).

Is it ***difficult*** **to learn** Italian? – I find it ***easy*** **to understand** but ***hard*** **to speak.**
It's ***important*** **to practise** a lot if you want to learn a language.

Wie im Deutschen kannst du den Infinitiv auch nach bestimmten Adjektiven benutzen, mit denen du etwas beurteilst, z. B. ***easy, hard, difficult, important, useful***.

People all over the world need English. Why do you think these people need it?
Diese Ausdrücke helfen dir:

fly a plane — explain things to tourists ✓ — work with computers
telephone people abroad — interview people from different countries

A tourist guide needs it to explain things to tourists.

A secretary needs it to telephone people abroad.

A pilot needs it to fly a plane.

A computer operator needs it to work with computers.

A reporter needs it to interview people from different countries.

4. Der Infinitiv nach Fragewörtern

Do you know **how to open** this door?
(Weißt du, wie man diese Tür öffnet?)
Could you show me **where to put** my bike?
(…, wo ich mein Rad abstellen kann?)
Please wait here. I'll tell you **when to come** in.
(…, wann du hereinkommen sollst.)
Please help me. I don't know **what to do.**
(Ich weiß nicht, was ich tun soll.)

Im Englischen kannst du nach einem Fragewort wie ***how, where, when, what*** einfach einen Infinitiv benutzen. Im Deutschen ist es viel umständlicher: Man muss einen Nebensatz verwenden.

Peter is unhappy. His parents always tell him what to do. *Welche Vorschriften machen Peters Eltern ihrem Sohn? Bilde Sätze mit* how, what, when, where *und Infinitiv.*

'Put on your anorak.'

They tell him what to put on.

They tell him what to read.

'Don't read so many comics. Read this.'

'Don't do your homework here. Do it in your bedroom.'

They tell him where to do his homework.

They tell him when to be back.

'Be back by seven.'

'Don't eat so fast.'
'Don't sit like that. Sit straight.'

They tell him how to sit and how to eat.

They tell him when to go to bed.

'It's time for you to go to bed.'

18 Die *ing*-Form

Das Gerund

1. Die *ing*-Form als Subjekt und nach bestimmten Verben

Music	is fun.
Singing	is fun.
Playing the guitar	is fun.

My favourite hobby ***is* collecting** stamps.
Do you ***like* reading** ***magazines?***
***I enjoy* jogging** but I ***hate* going** for walks.

Die ***ing***-Form des Verbs können wir im Satz wie ein Hauptwort (z. B. ***music***) verwenden.
In diesen Beispielen ist die ***ing***-Form Subjekt.

Die ***ing***-Form steht auch nach ***be*** und nach Verben, die eine Vorliebe oder Abneigung ausdrücken:
like, love, enjoy, hate.

Aufgepasst!

Do you ***like*** listening to pop records?

I ***love*** going to rock concerts.

Would you ***like*** to listen to my new pop record?

I***'d love*** to go to the rock concert tonight, but I haven't got time.

die ***ing***-Form? | der Infinitiv?

Nach ***like*** und ***love*** ohne ***would*** steht die ing-Form, weil diese Verben ohne ***would*** eine Vorliebe ausdrücken.

Nach ***would like*** und ***would love*** steht der Infinitiv, weil ***would like*** und ***would love*** einen Wunsch ausdrücken. (Vgl. S. 63.)

einen Wunsch? | eine Vorliebe?

Beachte die Schreibung der *ing*-Form bei manchen Verben:

swim **swimming** dance **dancing** lie **lying**

(Vgl. S. 11.)

What about you? *Nenne ein paar Tätigkeiten, die* **du** *interessant, langweilig, schön, schrecklich, amüsant, leicht, schwierig usw. findest. Hier sind ein paar Ideen:*
go to a museum, read the paper, meet friends, visit relatives, go shopping, learn to skate, . . .
interesting, boring, great, fun, nice, terrible, easy, hard, difficult, . . .

Going to a museum is ______________________

____

____

____

What do Susie, Eric, Brenda and Ken like or hate doing?

Susie	+	–	++	– –
Eric	– –	+	–	++
Brenda	++	– –	–	+
Ken	–	++	+	– –

 dancing

 playing table tennis

 swimming

 watching TV

\+ likes/enjoys
– doesn't like/doesn't enjoy
++ loves
– – hates

Susie likes dancing and she loves swimming.

She doesn't enjoy playing table tennis and she hates watching TV.

Eric hates dancing and he doesn't like/enjoy swimming.

He likes/enjoys playing table tennis and he loves watching TV.

Brenda loves dancing and she likes/enjoys watching TV.

She hates playing table tennis and she doesn't like/enjoy swimming.

Ken doesn't like/enjoy dancing and he hates watching TV.

He likes/enjoys swimming and he loves playing table tennis.

2. Die *ing*-Form nach Verhältniswörtern

Paul ***is very interested in* travelling.**
I***'m not very good at* reading** road maps.
A lot of people ***are afraid of* flying.**
We***'re looking forward to* going** to the seaside.
Why do you keep your bike beside your bed? –
Because I***'m tired of* walking** in my sleep.

Die ***ing***-Form steht auch nach Verhältniswörtern wie ***in, of, at, to.*** Wir verwenden sie z. B. nach folgenden Ausdrücken:
be interested in, be good at, be afraid of, look forward to (sich auf etwas freuen), ***be tired of.***

Diese jungen Leute wissen schon, was sie einmal werden wollen. Kannst du dir denken, welches ihre Hauptgründe sind? Folgende Wörter helfen dir:

be good, be interested, enjoy, like
be at sea, help people, meet people, organize, repair things, work outside, work with wood

Jane wants to be a nurse. She is interested in helping people.

Tim wants to be a gardener. He likes/enjoys working outside.

Jodie wants to be a mechanic. She is good at repairing things.

Eric wants to be a sailor. He likes/enjoys being at sea.

Roger wants to be a carpenter. He is good at working with wood.

Fiona wants to be a hotel manager. She is good at organizing, and she is interested in meeting people.

3. Weitere Verben und Ausdrücke mit *ing*-Form

***Stop* talking** and ***start* working.**
Have you ***finished* writing** your letter?
We ***went on* walking** although we were tired.
I can't work if you ***keep (on)* shouting.**
***What about* going** for a picnic? – Great! When?
Have you heard about the rich film star? She has four cars, one ***for* driving** in each direction *(Himmelsrichtung).*

Die *ing*-Form benutzen wir auch nach
- ***start, begin, finish, stop, go on, keep (on)*** (um Beginn, Ende oder Fortdauer einer Handlung zu bezeichnen)
- ***What about ... ?*** (um Vorschläge zu machen)
- ***for*** (um einen Zweck zu bezeichnen).

Was sagen diese Leute? Um die Sätze zu ergänzen, brauchst du folgende Verben und Ausdrücke:
finish, go on, keep, stop, what about
read, shout, go, play, tear (up) [tɛə] *(zerreißen)*

Please stop shouting.
I haven't even touched your tooth yet.
– But you're standing on my foot!

Have you finished reading that paper?
– Yes, you can have it.

What about going to the cinema?
– Are there any good films on?

Shall we go on playing?
– No, let's stop.

This is the tenth ticket you've bought.
– I know, but a girl in there keeps tearing them up.

Can you say what these things are **used for**?
Du brauchst folgende Verben: draw, look at, open, play

1. This is used for opening tins.
2. This is used for looking at small things.
3. This is used for drawing lines.
4. This is used for playing tennis.

19 Relativsätze

	Hauptwort	Relativsatz
This is	***the girl***	**who/that won the first prize.**
I don't like	***people***	**who/that are always late.**
Let's take	***the first bus***	**which/that goes to town.**
Are these	***the budgies***	**which/that you bought yesterday?**
Is this	***the man***	**whose dog bit you?**
	(... der Mann,	**dessen** Hund ...)
Do you know	***the people***	**whose house burnt down?**
	(... die Leute,	**deren** Haus niedergebrannt ist?)

Mit einem Relativsatz kannst du erklären, wen oder was genau du eigentlich mit einer Bezeichnung wie ***the girl, people, the first bus, the budgies*** meinst.
Die meisten Relativsätze beginnen mit ***who, which*** oder ***that.***

Es gibt auch Relativsätze mit ***whose.***
Sie entsprechen deutschen Relativsätzen mit ***dessen*** oder ***deren***.

Schau dir die Beispielsätze oben noch einmal an und finde heraus, wann man **who, which** *oder* **that** *verwendet:*

who nur bei Personen, z. B. the girl, people

which nur bei Sachen und bei Tieren, z. B. the first bus, the budgies

that sowohl bei Personen als auch bei Sachen und Tieren

"Of course I remember you – you're the boy whose name I always forget."

Ergänze die folgenden Fragen durch who, which *oder* that.
Bestimmt weißt du auch die Antworten.

What's the English word for . . .

. . . a person who lives in Spain? – A Spaniard.

. . . a man who/that brings your food to you in a restaurant? – A waiter.

. . . the thing which/that you use when it rains? – An umbrella.

. . . a book which/that tells you the English for German words? – A dictionary.

. . . the people who/that live near you? – Your neighbours.

. . . an animal which/that lives in Australia and can jump very high. – A kangaroo.

"Okay, which of you is the one they call 'Old-One-Eyed-Dog-Face'?

In der Umgangssprache wird das Relativpronomen im Englischen oft weggelassen.

Welches Relativpronomen könnte man in den beiden Beispielen unten einfügen?

What is smaller than an insect's mouth?
– The food it eats.

→ The food which/that it eats.

→ Okay, which of you is the one who/that they call 'Old-One-Eyed-Dog-Face'?

20 Die Steigerung von Adjektiven

Die Steigerung von Eigenschaftswörtern

This watch is **cheap**.

This one is even **cheaper**.

This one is the **cheapest** of all.

This bike is very **expensive**.

This one is even **more expensive**.

This one is the **most expensive** in the shop.

Adjektive (z. B. ***cheap*** oder ***expensive***) haben jeweils zwei Steigerungsformen ***(cheaper – cheapest, more expensive – most expensive)***. Mit diesen Steigerungsformen können wir Vergleiche ausdrücken.

Es gibt zwei Arten der Steigerung:

1. Wir hängen _-er_ oder _-est_ an das Adjektiv.
2. Wir stellen _more_ oder _most_ davor.

1. Die Steigerung mit *-er/-est*

fast	–	fast**er**	–	the fast**est**
tall	–	tall**er**	–	the tall**est**
easy	–	easi**er**	–	the easi**est**
crazy	–	crazi**er**	–	the crazi**est**
good	–	**better**	–	the **best**
bad	–	**worse**	–	the **worst**

Einsilbige Adjektive werden mit ***-er/-est*** gesteigert, außerdem auch mehrsilbige Adjektive, die mit ***-y*** enden.

⚠ ***Good*** und ***bad*** haben unregelmäßige Steigerungsformen.

Jetzt musst du nur noch ein paar Schreibregeln beachten, wenn du ***-er*** oder ***-est*** anhängst:

nice – nicer – nicest large – larger – largest

Wenn das Adjektiv auf _e_ endet, hänge ich nur _r_ oder _st_ an.

sad – sadder – saddest wet – wetter – wettest

big – bigger – biggest thin – thinner – thinnest

Ein einfacher Mitlaut wie ***d, t, g*** oder ***n*** wird vor ***-er*** und ***-est*** _verdoppelt / zu dd, tt usw._, wenn ein kurzer Selbstlaut wie ***a, e, i, o, u*** [æ, e, ɪ, ɒ, ʊ] vorangeht.

heavy – heavier – heaviest happy – happier – happiest

Das _y_ am Ende wird vor ***-er*** und ***-est*** zu _i_.

2. Die Steigerung mit *more/most*

interesting	– **more** interesting	– the **most** interesting
boring	– **more** boring	– the **most** boring
useful	– **more** useful	– the **most** useful

Die meisten mehrsilbigen Adjektive werden mit ***more/most*** gesteigert (außer Adjektiven, die mit ***-y*** enden).

Kannst du diese Anzeige eines großen Kaufhauses ergänzen? Du brauchst dazu die 2. Steigerungsform der Adjektive (mit -est *oder* most*).*

Looking for anything special? We can help you!

Do you want … *We have*

Do you want	We have
a cheap calculator?	the cheapest calculators ...
a nice T-shirt?	the nicest T-shirts ...
a funny sticker?	the funniest stickers ...
a beautiful poster?	the most beautiful posters ...
a powerful drill?	the most powerful drills ...
a big wardrobe?	the biggest wardrobes ...
modern furniture?	the most modern furniture ...
good quality?	the best quality ...
low prices?	the lowest prices ...
friendly shop assistants?	the friendliest shop assistants ...
perfect service?	the most perfect service

in town!

Have a laugh!

What word becomes shorter when you add two letters to it?
– Add 'er' to 'short' and it becomes 'shorter'.

*****

Teacher: What is more important, the sun or the moon?
Effie: The moon, because it shines at night, when it's dark. The sun shines when it's light anyway.

Teacher: Susan, what is the highest form of animal life?
Susan: I think it's the giraffe.

*****

My mother has the worst memory in the world.
– Does she forget everything?
– No, she remembers everything.

memory Gedächtnis

3. Vergleiche mit *as* und *than*

Bill is **as**	***heavy***	**as**	Joe.	(… **so** schwer **wie** …)
Big Ben is **as**	***famous***	**as**	the Tower.	(… **so** berühmt **wie** …)
Jill is**n't as**	***heavy***	**as**	Joe.	(… nicht **so** schwer **wie** …)
The Clyde is**n't as**	***famous***	**as**	the Thames.	(nicht … **so** berühmt **wie** …)
Bob is	***heavier***	**than**	Joe.	(… schwer**er als** …)
Loch Ness is **more**	***famous***	**than**	Loch Linnhe.	(… berühmt**er als** …)

Lies dir die folgenden Sätze durch und ergänze die Vergleiche.
Die Adjektive in Klammern helfen dir.

Debbie is 1.65 m, Sheila is 1.70.	Debbie isn't as tall as Sheila. (tall)
Kevin got 16 marks out of 20 in a test, Penny got 18.	Penny's marks were better than Kevin's. (good)
Athens is about 27° C in the summer, Madrid is about 25° C.	Madrid isn't as hot as Athens. (hot)
Stella and Steve were both born on 1st September 1981.	Steve is as old as Stella. (old)
Britain won 10 medals in the sports contest. France won 12.	Britain wasn't as successful as France. (successful)
40 % of the people want Jackson for President, 40 % want Brown.	Brown is as popular as Jackson. (popular)

Sue and Alan aren't **as** old **as *me***.
(… nicht so alt **wie *ich***.)
I'm 6 months older **than *her*** and one year older **than *him***.
(… älter **als *sie*** … … älter **als *er***.)

Nach ***as*** und ***than*** sagt man gewöhnlich:
me, him, her, us, them
(nicht *I, he, she, we, they!*).

Übersetze die folgenden Sätze.
Achte dabei vor allem auf die Übersetzung der persönlichen Fürwörter ich, er, sie, wir.

1. Meine Schwester ist ein Jahr älter als ich, aber ich bin so groß wie sie.

   My sister is a/one year older than me, but I'm as tall as her.

2. Peter wollte sich das letzte Stück Kuchen nehmen, aber ich war schneller als er.

   Peter wanted to take the last piece of cake, but I was faster than him.

3. Wir haben das Spiel gegen die "Rovers" verloren. Wir waren besser als sie, aber sie hatten mehr Glück als wir. *(Glück haben: be lucky)*

   We lost the match against the "Rovers". We were better than them, but they were luckier than us.

21 Adjektiv oder Adverb?

Eigenschaftswort oder Umstandswort?

Was heißt „billig“ auf Englisch?

Die Frage ist nicht so leicht, wie sie scheint.
Du denkst natürlich sofort an “cheap”.
Aber Vorsicht: Es kann auch “cheaply” heißen:

Our ticket was **cheap.**
We travelled **cheaply.**

Unsere Fahrkarte war **billig**.
Wir reisten **billig.**

Im Englischen ist es wichtig, zwischen Adjektiven (wie ***cheap***) und Adverbien (wie ***cheaply***) zu unterscheiden.

Adjektiv	Adverb
We got a **cheap *ticket*.** Our ticket ***was* cheap.** Please ***keep* quiet** when we're in the museum. Bob ***got* angry** when I asked him to leave. I ***feel* terrible** today. You ***look* nice** in that dress.	You can ***travel* cheaply** with Inter-rail. Please ***leave* quietly** when you've finished. He ***slammed*** the door **angrily** when he went out. My head ***hurts* terribly.** You***'ve done*** your hair **nicely.**
Mit einem Adjektiv kannst du eine **Eigenschaft** beschreiben: wie eine Person oder Sache **ist**. Vor einem Hauptwort (z. B. ***ticket***) und nach folgenden Verben musst du deshalb ein Adjektiv verwenden: ***be*** sein — ***look*** aussehen ***stay/keep*** bleiben — ***sound*** klingen ***become/get*** werden — ***smell*** riechen ***feel*** sich fühlen — ***taste*** schmecken	Mit einem Adverb kannst du die **Art und Weise** beschreiben, wie jemand etwas **tut** oder wie etwas **geschieht.** Nach den meisten Verben musst du deshalb ein Adverb verwenden. Wie die Beispiele zeigen, werden die meisten Adverbien so gebildet: Adjektiv + ly .

Aufgepasst!

This exercise looks **easy**. I think I can do it **easily.**
Sue was smiling **happily**. “Why are you so **happy**?” I asked her.

You screamed **terribly** last night. – I had a **terrible** dream.
Although Mrs Carr is rich, she wears **simple** clothes and lives very **simply**.

Jean plays the violin very **well**.
She's **good** at sports, too.

Mrs Cole has a **fast** car. But she never drives very **fast.**
If you want to catch the **early** train, you'll have to get up **early.**

Adjektiv	Adverb
easy	easily
happy	happily
terrible	terribly
simple	simply
good	well
fast	fast
early	early

y wird vor ***ly*** zu i .

le wird vor ***ly*** weg- gelassen .

Das Adverb well ist eine unregelmäßige Form.

Bei ***fast*** und ***early*** wird nichts angehängt.

Entscheide, ob du hier ein Adjektiv oder ein Adverb einsetzen musst.
Benutze folgende Adjektive und die entsprechenden Adverbien:

bad, careful, early, fast, good, heavy, nice, slow, terrible

You've got to drive very ___slowly___ here.

Don't drive too ___fast___.

She can't sleep any more,

but it's too ___early___ to get up.

The 9.20 is a ___slow___ train.

The 9.30 is a ___fast___ one.

TRAIN TIMES		
Manchester	9.20	9.30
Sheffield	11.20	10.25

Shall we go for a walk?

That's a ___good___ idea.

She sings quite ___nicely/well___.

Yes, she's got a ___nice/good___ voice.

Ooh! This egg smells ___bad/terrible___.

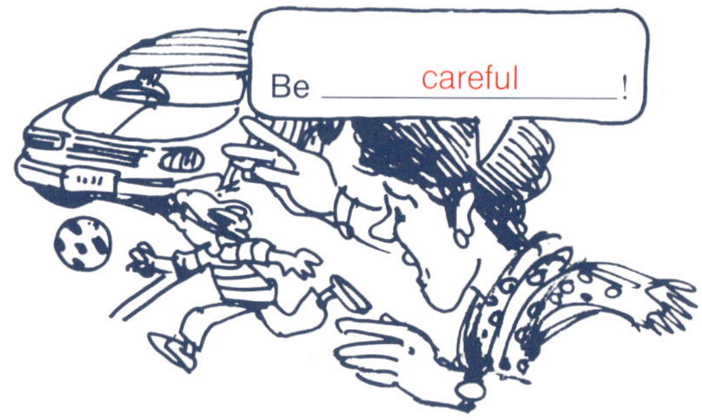

Be ___careful___!

LIVERPOOL 0 LEEDS 6

Liverpool played ___badly___.

Leeds played ___well___.

This shop opens very ___early___.

Drive ___carefully/slowly___, please.

I miss you ___terribly___.

It's too ___heavy___.

I've made a ___terrible / bad___ mistake.

It will rain ___heavily___ all day.

22 *Some* und *any*

und ihre Zusammensetzungen

1. Verwendung in bejahten und verneinten Aussagen

Bejahter Satz: *some, someone* usw.	**Verneinter Satz: *any, anyone* usw.**
There's **some *milk*** in the fridge. (Im Kühlschrank ist etwas Milch.) I've bought **some *sweets***. (Ich habe ein paar Bonbons gekauft.)	I do**n't** want **any *milk***. I **never** drink **any**. (Ich möchte keine Milch. Ich trinke nie welche.) Everybody drank a lot of tea, but **nobody** ate **any *biscuits***. (... niemand aß Kekse.)
Wenn du von einer unbestimmten Menge (z. B. Milch) oder Anzahl (z. B. Bonbons) sprichst, musst du in bejahten Sätzen ***some*** benutzen.	In verneinten Sätzen musst du ***any*** benutzen. ⚠ Dies gilt auch für Sätze, die durch Wörter wie ***never*** oder ***nobody*** verneint werden.
There's **someone/somebody** at the front door. Let's have **something** to eat and drink. It's very noisy here. Let's go **somewhere** else.	I'm new here. I do**n't** know **anyone/anybody** yet. I **never** eat **anything** between breakfast and lunch. Where's Bill? I ca**n't** find him **anywhere.**
In bejahten Sätzen musst du Zusammensetzungen mit ***some*** benutzen: ***someone*** oder ***somebody*** – (irgend) jemand ***something*** – (irgend) etwas ***somewhere*** – irgendwo(hin)	In verneinten Sätzen musst du Zusammensetzungen mit ***any*** benutzen. Merke dir: ***not + anyone/anybody*** – niemand ***not + anything*** – nichts ***not + anywhere*** – nirgendwo(hin)

Carol und ihre Schwester Ann sind heute mit dem Bus in die Stadt gefahren, um Weihnachtseinkäufe zu machen. Ergänze ihren Dialog. Du musst zwischen folgenden Wörtern entscheiden:
some, any, someone *oder* somebody, anyone *oder* anybody, something, anything, somewhere, anywhere

Carol: They haven't got ___any___ nice Christmas cards here. Let's look ___somewhere___ else.

Ann: I've had enough. I don't want to go ___anywhere___ else. I'm tired and hungry. Let's get ___something___ to eat. I haven't eaten ___anything___ since breakfast.

Carol: Okay, let's buy ___some___ sandwiches over there. They're 75p each.

Ann: Oh, dear! I haven't got ___any___ money left *(übrig)*. How much have you left?

Carol: Just 70p.

Ann: But our bus tickets back cost 80p each.

Carol: So we'll have to walk home, and we can't buy ___any___ sandwiches.

Ann: We could telephone home and ask ___someone/somebody___ to come by car and fetch us.

Carol: You know there isn't ___anyone/anybody___ at home at the moment. They've gone to see Granny and won't be back until six.

Ann: Let's try and hitchhike, then. I'm sure ___someone/somebody___ will give us a lift.

2. Verwendung in Fragen

Bitten und Angebote: ***some, someone*** usw.	„Echte" Fragen: ***any, anyone*** usw.
Can you lend me **some** money, please? Could **someone** answer the phone, please? Would you like **something** to drink? I'm tired. – Shall we sit down **somewhere**?	Have you got **any** money on you? Did **anyone** call while I was out? Is there **anything** to drink in the fridge? Have you seen my bag **anywhere?**
Wir benutzen oft Fragesätze, wenn wir um etwas bitten, etwas anbieten oder etwas vorschlagen wollen. In solchen Fragen musst du ***some*** oder seine Zusammensetzungen verwenden.	Wenn du eine Frage stellst, weil du etwas nicht weißt und eine Auskunft haben möchtest (also in „echten" Fragen), musst du ***any*** oder seine Zusammensetzungen verwenden.

Was sagen die Leute in den folgenden Szenen?
Ergänze die Sätze durch some, any *oder eine Zusammensetzung mit* some *oder* any.

Can I have ___some___ chocolate, please?

Does ___anyone/anybody___ speak Italian?

Shall we stop and have a break ___somewhere___ ?

Have you found ___anything___ nice?

Have you got ___any___ letters for me today?

Can ___someone/somebody___ open the door for me, please?

I can't find my walkman. Have you seen it ___anywhere___ ?

Would you like ___something___ to drink?

Liste der wichtigsten unregelmäßigen Verben

Hier haben wir drei unterschiedliche Formen des gleichen Verbs:
- den Infinitiv (die Grundform): ***(to) see***
- die ***past-simple***-Form: ***saw***
- das ***past participle: seen***

Wenn du diese drei Formen kennst, kannst du alle Zeitformen dieses Verbs bilden. Mit dem ***past participle*** kannst du z. B. das ***present perfect (I have seen)*** und alle Zeitformen des Passivs bilden (***he was seen, he has been seen,*** usw.).

In der folgenden Liste kannst du diese drei Formen der wichtigsten unregelmäßigen Verben nachschlagen. Am besten lernst du sie auswendig.

Bei den regelmäßigen Verben ist dies nicht notwendig, da wir beim ***past simple*** und beim ***past participle*** nur die Endung ***-ed*** an den Infinitiv anhängen müssen.
Vergleiche: I've got to **finish**. – I **finished** yesterday. – I haven't **finished** yet.

Infinitiv		***Past simple***		***Past participle***		
be	[bi:]	was, were	[wɒz, wɜ:]	been	[bi:n]	sein
beat	[bi:t]	beat	[bi:t]	beaten	[ˈbi:tn]	schlagen
become	[bɪˈkʌm]	became	[bɪˈkeɪm]	become	[bɪˈkʌm]	werden
begin	[bɪˈgɪn]	began	[bɪˈgæn]	begun	[bɪˈgʌn]	beginnen
bite	[baɪt]	bit	[bɪt]	bitten	[ˈbɪtn]	beißen
blow	[bləʊ]	blew	[blu:]	blow	[bləʊn]	blasen, wehen
break	[breɪk]	broke	[brəʊk]	broken	[ˈbrəʊkn]	(zer)brechen
bring	[brɪŋ]	brought	[brɔ:t]	brought	[brɔ:t]	bringen
build	[bɪld]	built	[bɪlt]	built	[bɪlt]	bauen
buy	[baɪ]	bought	[bɔ:t]	bought	[bɔ:t]	kaufen
catch	[kætʃ]	caught	[kɔ:t]	caught	[kɔ:t]	fangen
choose	[tʃu:z]	chose	[tʃəʊz]	chosen	[ˈtʃəʊzn]	(aus)wählen
come	[kʌm]	came	[keɪm]	come	[kʌm]	kommen
cost	[kɒst]	cost	[kɒst]	cost	[kɒst]	kosten
cut	[kʌt]	cut	[kʌt]	cut	[kʌt]	schneiden
do	[du:]	did	[dɪd]	done	[dʌn]	tun, machen
draw	[drɔ:]	drew	[dru:]	drawn	[drɔ:n]	zeichnen; ziehen
drink	[drɪŋk]	drank	[dræŋk]	drunk	[drʌŋk]	trinken
drive	[draɪv]	drove	[drəʊv]	driven	[ˈdrɪvn]	fahren; antreiben
eat	[i:t]	ate	[et]	eaten	[ˈi:tn]	essen
fall	[fɔ:l]	fell	[fel]	fallen	[ˈfɔ:ln]	fallen
feed	[fi:d]	fed	[fed]	fed	[fed]	füttern
feel	[fi:l]	felt	[felt]	felt	[felt]	(sich) fühlen
fight	[faɪt]	fought	[fɔ:t]	fought	[fɔ:t]	kämpfen
find	[faɪnd]	found	[faʊnd]	found	[faʊnd]	finden
fly	[flaɪ]	flew	[flu:]	flown	[fləʊn]	fliegen
forget	[fəˈget]	forgot	[fəˈgɒt]	forgotten	[fəˈgɒtn]	vergessen
get	[get]	got	[gɒt]	got	[gɒt]	holen; bekommen; werden; gelangen
give	[gɪv]	gave	[geɪv]	given	[ˈgɪvn]	geben
go	[gəʊ]	went	[went]	gone	[gɒn]	gehen; fahren
grow	[grəʊ]	grew	[gru:]	grown	[grəʊn]	wachsen; züchten, anbauen

Infinitiv		*Past simple*		*Past participle*		
hang	[hæŋ]	hung	[hʌŋ]	hung	[hʌŋ]	hängen
have	[hæv]	had	[hæd]	had	[hæd]	haben
hear	[hɪə]	heard	[hɜ:d]	heard	[hɜ:d]	hören
hit	[hɪt]	hit	[hɪt]	hit	[hɪt]	(auf)schlagen
hold	[həʊld]	held	[held]	held	[held]	halten
hurt	[hɜ:t]	hurt	[hɜ:t]	hurt	[hɜ:t]	verletzen; schmerzen
keep	[ki:p]	kept	[kept]	kept	[kept]	behalten; halten; bleiben
know	[nəʊ]	knew	[nju:]	known	[nəʊn]	wissen, kennen
lead	[li:d]	led	[led]	led	[led]	führen
leave	[li:v]	left	[left]	left	[left]	verlassen, (zurück-) lassen; abfahren
lend	[lend]	lent	[lent]	lent	[lent]	leihen
let	[let]	let	[let]	let	[let]	lassen
lie	[laɪ]	lay	[leɪ]	lain	[leɪn]	liegen
lose	[lu:z]	lost	[lɒst]	lost	[lɒst]	verlieren
make	[meɪk]	made	[meɪd]	made	[meɪd]	machen
mean	[mi:n]	meant	[ment]	meant	[ment]	meinen; bedeuten
meet	[mi:t]	met	[met]	met	[met]	treffen; abholen
pay	[peɪ]	paid	[peɪd]	paid	[peɪd]	bezahlen
put	[pʊt]	put	[pʊt]	put	[pʊt]	stellen, legen, setzen
read	[ri:d]	read	[red]	read	[red]	lesen
ride	[raɪd]	rode	[rəʊd]	ridden	[ˈrɪdn]	reiten, fahren
ring	[rɪŋ]	rang	[ræŋ]	rung	[rʌŋ]	klingeln
run	[rʌn]	ran	[ræn]	run	[rʌn]	laufen, rennen
say	[seɪ]	said	[sed]	said	[sed]	sagen
see	[si:]	saw	[sɔ:]	seen	[si:n]	sehen
sell	[sel]	sold	[səʊld]	sold	[səʊld]	verkaufen
send	[send]	sent	[sent]	sent	[sent]	schicken
set	[set]	set	[set]	set	[set]	stellen
shake	[ʃeɪk]	shook	[ʃʊk]	shaken	[ˈʃeɪkn]	schütteln
shine	[ʃaɪn]	shone	[ʃɒn]	shone	[ʃɒn]	glänzen; scheinen
shoot	[ʃu:t]	shot	[ʃɒt]	shot	[ʃɒt]	schießen
show	[ʃəʊ]	showed	[ʃəʊd]	shown	[ʃəʊn]	zeigen
shut	[ʃʌt]	shut	[ʃʌt]	shut	[ʃʌt]	schließen
sing	[sɪŋ]	sang	[sæŋ]	sung	[sʌŋ]	singen
sink	[sɪŋk]	sank	[sæŋk]	sunk	[sʌŋk]	sinken
sit	[sɪt]	sat	[sæt]	sat	[sæt]	sitzen
sleep	[sli:p]	slept	[slept]	slept	[slept]	schlafen
speak	[spi:k]	spoke	[spəʊk]	spoken	[ˈspəʊkn]	sprechen
spend	[spend]	spent	[spent]	spent	[spent]	verbringen; ausgeben
stand	[stænd]	stood	[stʊd]	stood	[stʊd]	stehen
steal	[sti:l]	stole	[stəʊl]	stolen	[ˈstəʊln]	stehlen
swim	[swɪm]	swam	[swæm]	swum	[swʌm]	schwimmen
take	[teɪk]	took	[tʊk]	taken	[ˈteɪkn]	bringen; nehmen
teach	[ti:tʃ]	taught	[tɔ:t]	taught	[tɔ:t]	lehren, unterrichten
tear	[teə]	tore	[tɔ:]	torn	[tɔ:n]	zerreißen
tell	[tel]	told	[təʊld]	told	[təʊld]	erzählen, berichten
think	[θɪnk]	thought	[θɔ:t]	thought	[θɔ:t]	denken, glauben
throw	[θrəʊ]	threw	[θru:]	thrown	[θrəʊn]	werfen
under-stand	[ʌndə-ˈstænd]	under-stood	[ʌndə-ˈstʊd]	under-stood	[ʌndəˈstʊd]	verstehen
wake up	[weɪk‿ˈʌp]	woke up	[wəʊk‿ˈʌp]	woken up	[ˈwəʊkn‿ˈʌp]	aufwachen
wear	[weə]	wore	[wɔ:]	worn	[wɔ:n]	tragen *(Kleidung)*
win	[wɪn]	won	[wʌn]	won	[wʌn]	gewinnen
write	[raɪt]	wrote	[rəʊt]	written	[ˈrɪtn]	schreiben